Soups and Starters

Marguerite Patten

Hamlyn
London · New York · Sydney · Toronto

Published by
The Hamlyn Publishing Group Limited
London · New York · Sydney · Toronto
Astronaut House, Feltham, Middlesex, England
© Copyright The Hamlyn Publishing Group Limited 1973
ISBN 0 600 30210 5
Printed in England by Sir Joseph Causton and Sons Limited
Line drawings by John Scott Martin
Set 'Monophoto' by Page Bros (Norwich) Limited

Contents

Useful facts and figures

Note on metrication

In this book quantities are given in both Imperial and metric measures. Exact conversion from Imperial to metric does not always give very convenient working quantities so for greater convenience and ease of working we have taken an equivalent of 25 grammes/millilitres to the ounce/fluid ounce. 1 oz. is exactly 28·35 g. and $\frac{1}{4}$ pint (5 fl. oz.) is 142 ml., so you will see that by using the unit of 25 you will get a slightly smaller result than the Imperial measures would give.

Occasionally, for example in a basic recipe such as a Victoria sandwich made with 4 oz. flour, butter and sugar and 2 eggs, we have rounded the conversion up to give a more generous result. For larger amounts where the exact conversion is not critical, for instance in soups or stews, we have used kilogrammes and fractions (1 kg. equals 2·2 lb.) and litres and fractions (1 litre equals 1·76 pints). All recipes have been individually converted so that each recipe preserves the correct proportions.

Oven temperatures

The following chart gives the Celsius (Centigrade) equivalents recommended by the Electricity Council.

Description	Fahrenheit	Celsius	Gas Mark
Very cool	225	110	$\frac{1}{4}$
	250	130	$\frac{1}{2}$
Cool	275	140	1
	300	150	2
Moderate	325	170	3
	350	180	4
Moderately hot	375	190	5
	400	200	6
Hot	425	220	7
	450	230	8
Very hot	475	240	9

Introduction

Have you ever planned a 'make-do' family meal, then had unexpected guests? This has happened to me on many occasions, as I am sure it has to you.

I hope the recipes in this book provide the solution to this problem. It contains a selection of soups, dips, starters and more formal hors d'oeuvre and with one of these dishes you turn the plain meal into something more sophisticated.

I have a particular fondness for soups; I find if I am tired, and not particularly hungry, that a good soup revives me and satisfies my appetite. I find I can often make use of left-overs in a soup. In winter time a hot soup is an obvious choice, but do try cold soups in warmer weather, they are most refreshing.

Perhaps you have never made a dip; this is a very modern approach to catering. Dips are splendid when you entertain, for they immediately create a festive atmosphere. I find that children, as well as adults, enjoy a savoury dip, and everyone appreciates the tempting appearance of the trays of colourful ingredients to dip into the creamy flavoursome mixture.

There are no limitations on the kind of food with which to start a meal and this section of the book gives recipes with fruit, fish, eggs and cheese as well as salads and vegetables.

If you start a meal well, then you create the right atmosphere for everyone to enjoy the food, and I hope you will find this book gives you first-class 'starters'.

Marguerite Patten

Tomato vegetable broth

Cooking time: 30 minutes
Preparation time: 20 minutes
Main cooking utensil: saucepan
Serves: 6

Imperial	Metric
2 lb. tomatoes including 8 oz. very small ones	1 kg. tomatoes including 200 g. very small ones
4 medium-sized onions	4 medium-sized onions
2 cloves garlic (optional)	2 cloves garlic (optional)
4 tablespoons oil	4 tablespoons oil
3-inch piece cucumber	7-cm. piece cucumber
water and 2 chicken stock cubes	water and 2 chicken stock cubes
seasoning	seasoning
1 green pepper	1 green pepper
about ¼ small cabbage	about ¼ small cabbage

1. Chop 1½ lb. (¾ kg.) large tomatoes, do not skin them for the soup is generally sieved.

2. Peel and chop 3 of the onions and crush the garlic cloves.

3. Heat 3 tablespoons oil and toss the tomatoes and onions in this, then add the stock, or water and stock cubes, season well and simmer for 15–20 minutes. Sieve and put on one side.

4. Slice the remaining onion, the cucumber and the pepper, discarding core and seeds, and shred the cabbage.

5. Toss in remaining oil for a few minutes, add the remaining skinned tomatoes, heat for a few minutes only.

6. Add the sieved tomatoes and heat together gently until the soup is very hot. Serve with crusty bread.

Note: Tomato soup is a favourite in Portugal, and tomatoes are used in soups with a variety of ingredients.

Variation
Add sliced hard-boiled eggs.

Browned onion soup

Cooking time: 35 minutes
Preparation time: 10 minutes
Main cooking utensil: saucepan
Serves: 4

Imperial	Metric
4 medium-sized onions	4 medium-sized onions
2 oz. butter	50 g. butter
2 pints good brown stock (see note)	generous litre good brown stock (see note)
seasoning	seasoning
4 rounds French bread	4 rounds French bread
2–3 oz. Gruyère cheese, grated	50–75 g. Gruyère cheese, grated

1. Cut the onions into thin rounds.
2. Fry in the hot butter until pale gold; do not allow to become too dark.
3. Add the stock and seasoning and simmer for approximately 20 minutes.
4. If using a 'cook and serve' dish as shown, add the rounds of bread (which can be toasted) to the soup in the pan, sprinkle on the grated cheese and brown under the grill. If preferred, put the bread into 4 soup bowls, add the soup and cheese and brown.

Note: Stock should be made with beef bones and can be flavoured with yeast or beef extract for additional flavour. Do not exceed the given amount of cheese and do not overcook.

Variations
Omit the bread or toast and the cheese and serve the soup topped with chopped parsley or chervil. Use a white stock and 1 pint (generous $\frac{1}{2}$ litre) stock and 1 pint (generous $\frac{1}{2}$ litre) milk. Cook as above, top with the cheese, but do not brown.

Vegetable chowder

Cooking time: 30 minutes
Preparation time: 15 minutes
Main cooking utensil: large saucepan
Serves: 4–5

Imperial	**Metric**
2–3 large leeks	2–3 large leeks
2 onions	2 onions
4 carrots	4 carrots
3–4 stalks celery	3–4 stalks celery
1 small turnip (optional)	1 small turnip (optional)
1 oz. butter	25 g. butter
2–3 oz. lean bacon, diced	50–75 g. lean bacon, diced
1 oz. flour	25 g. flour
1½ pints stock or water	¾ litre stock or water
seasoning	seasoning
3 oz. rice	75 g. rice
Topping:	*Topping:*
grated cheese	grated cheese

1. Dice the leeks, onions, carrots, celery and turnip.
2. Heat the butter in a saucepan and fry the diced bacon until crisp. Stir in the flour and cook for a few minutes.
3. Add the stock gradually and bring to the boil, stirring.
4. Add the vegetables and simmer until tender, seasoning well. Meanwhile boil the rice in salted water until tender. Drain and add to the chowder. Top with grated cheese and serve with hot rolls.

Note: The word chowder means a soup which is almost as thick and as filling as pot-au-feu. By adding cheese to vegetable chowder you can turn this into a complete and very satisfying meal.

Carrot soup

Cooking time: 2 hours
Preparation time: 15 minutes
Main cooking utensils: frying pan, saucepan
Serves: 4–5

Imperial
1 large onion
1½ oz. butter or margarine
2 pints white stock or
    water
1 lb. carrots, peeled and
    chopped
1 clove garlic, crushed
seasoning
1½ oz. flour
½ pint milk
parsley

Metric
1 large onion
40 g. butter or margarine
generous litre white stock or
    water
½ kg. carrots, peeled and
    chopped
1 clove garlic, crushed
seasoning
40 g. flour
250 ml. milk
parsley

1. Chop the onion and toss in the butter or margarine.
2. Add the white stock or water and the carrots with the garlic.
3. Season well, being particularly generous with pepper, and simmer for 30–40 minutes until the carrots are tender.
4. Blend the flour and milk and work until smooth. Bring to the boil, stirring constantly, and cook until thickened.
5. Sieve the carrot mixture, blend with the thickened milk. Reheat and top with chopped parsley.
6. Serve with fried bread croûtons.

Variation
To give more colour and flavour, add two skinned tomatoes and 2 teaspoons paprika. Fry the tomatoes with the onion at stage 1 and blend the paprika with the flour at stage 4.

Celery cream soup

Cooking time: 1½ hours
Preparation time: 20 minutes
Main cooking utensil: saucepan
Serves: 5–6

Imperial	Metric
2 onions	2 onions
2 oz. butter	50 g. butter
2 pints white stock or water and 2–3 chicken stock cubes	generous litre white stock or water and 2–3 chicken stock cubes
1 lb. celery, chopped	$\frac{1}{2}$ kg. celery, chopped
2–3 teaspoons soup seasoning	2–3 teaspoons soup seasoning
2 teaspoons paprika	2 teaspoons paprika
$\frac{1}{2}$–1 tablespoon tomato purée	$\frac{1}{2}$–1 tablespoon tomato purée
1 oz. flour	25 g. flour
$\frac{1}{4}$ pint thin cream or evaporated milk	125 ml. thin cream or evaporated milk
Garnish:	*Garnish:*
parsley	parsley

1. Chop the onions and fry in the butter until soft.

2. Add the white stock or water and stock cubes, the celery, soup seasoning, paprika and tomato purée.

3. Simmer for approximately 45 minutes then sieve the soup and reheat.

4. Blend the flour with the cream or evaporated milk. Stir into the hot soup and cook steadily until thickened. Do not cook too quickly.

5. Garnish with freshly chopped or dried parsley. If using the dried parsley, simmer in the soup for 5 minutes.

Turnip top soup

Cooking time: 35 minutes
Preparation time: 15 minutes
Main cooking utensils: saucepan, frying pan
Serves: 4–5

Imperial	Metric
8–12 oz. turnip tops	200–300 g. turnip tops
1 large onion	1 large onion
2 medium-sized potatoes	2 medium-sized potatoes
1½ oz. butter	40 g. butter
½ oz. flour	15 g. flour
1 teaspoon curry powder	1 teaspoon curry powder
2½ pints white stock or water and 2–3 chicken stock cubes	1¼ litres white stock or water and 2–3 chicken stock cubes
1½ oz. rice	40 g. rice
seasoning	seasoning
Garnish (optional):	*Garnish (optional):*
2 slices bread	2 slices bread
1–2 oz. butter or fat	25–50 g. butter or fat

1. Shred the turnip tops very finely, discarding any tough old leaves.
2. Chop the onion and dice the potatoes.
3. Heat the butter and fry the onion until tender but not brown.
4. Blend in the flour and the curry powder.
5. Add the stock or water and stock cubes and bring to the boil.
6. Add the potatoes and rice and season well. Cook steadily for 10 minutes. Add the turnip tops and continue cooking for a further 10–15 minutes.
7. If wished, dice 2 slices of bread and fry in 1–2 oz. (25–50 g.) butter or fat until crisp and golden. Put on the soup just before serving.

Variation
Chinese vegetable soup: Bring 1½ pints (generous ¾ litre) white stock to the boil. Add 8 oz. (200 g.) very finely chopped turnip top leaves and 3–4 oz. (75–100 g.) finely diced, lean pork. Simmer steadily until tender then add seasoning, pinch monosodium glutamate and 2 tablespoons sherry.

Dutch onion soup

Cooking time: 1 hour
Preparation time: 10 minutes
Main cooking utensil: saucepan, grill
Serves: 5–6

Imperial	Metric
1¼ lb. onions	generous ½ kg. onions
2 oz. butter	50 g. butter
1½ oz. flour	40 g. flour
2½ pints brown stock	1¼ litres brown stock
seasoning	seasoning
2–3 slices bread	2–3 slices bread
grated Gruyère, Dutch Gouda or Edam cheese	grated Gruyère, Dutch Gouda or Edam cheese

1. Peel and slice the onions and toss in the butter until soft but not browned.
2. Stir in the flour and cook for a few minutes then gradually blend in the brown stock.
3. Bring to the boil and cook until slightly thickened, season well. Reduce the heat and let the soup simmer for about 45 minutes, stirring from time to time.
4. Cut bread into shapes to fit the top of the soup tureen or bowl. Pour in the soup and top with the bread. Cover this with a good layer of grated Gruyère, Dutch Gouda or Edam cheese and brown under the grill.

Polish tomato soup

Cooking time: 45 minutes
Preparation time: 10 minutes
Main cooking utensil: saucepan
Serves: 4–6

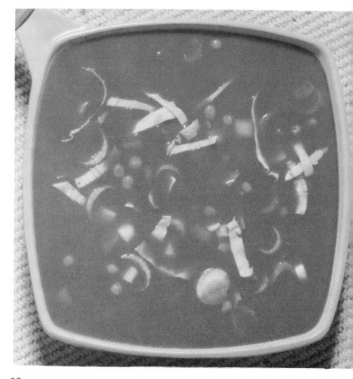

Imperial	Metric
1¼ lb. tomatoes	generous ½ kg. tomatoes
2 oz. fat or dripping	50 g. fat or dripping
1½ oz. potato or ordinary flour	40 g. potato or ordinary flour
2½ pints stock	scant 1½ litres stock
2–3 teaspoons sugar	2–3 teaspoons sugar
seasoning	seasoning

1. Skin the tomatoes and, if wished, deseed them. This makes a very smooth soup.

2. Fry the tomatoes in the fat or dripping until soft.

3. Blend in the flour, stock, sugar and seasoning; then bring to the boil and simmer for 30 minutes.

Variation

Add dried vegetables and cook these until soft (see picture) or add noodles.

Austrian tomato soup: Chop 1 carrot, 1 onion, 1 stick celery and toss in 2 oz. (50 g.) butter. Add 1¼ lb. (generous ½ kg.) tomatoes and cook for several minutes. Blend 1 oz. (25 g.) flour with 2 pints (generous litre) stock or water. Add to the vegetables with seasoning, a pinch paprika, 1 bay leaf, pinch marjoram and the juice and rind of 1 lemon. Simmer until tender, sieve and reheat. Stir in 2 oz. (50 g.) cooked rice before serving.

Clear tomato soup

Cooking time: 2 hours or see stage 2
Preparation time: 15 minutes
Main cooking utensil: saucepan
Serves: 5–6

Imperial	Metric
chicken carcass	chicken carcass
about 4 oz. bacon pieces	about 100 g. bacon pieces
1 or 2 onions	1 or 2 onions
bouquet garni	bouquet garni
seasoning	seasoning
4 large tomatoes	4 large tomatoes
sprig fresh thyme or ½ teaspoon powdered thyme	sprig fresh thyme or ½ teaspoon powdered thyme
1 bay leaf	1 bay leaf
pinch sugar (optional)	pinch sugar (optional)

1. Put the chicken carcass into the pan, add the bacon pieces, onions, herbs and seasoning.

2. Cook with water to cover for approximately 1½ hours in an ordinary saucepan or for 30 minutes in a pressure cooker at 15-lb. (7-kg.) pressure. Allow the pressure to drop at room temperature.

3. Strain the liquid carefully; for a clear soup without fat it is a good idea to let the strained liquid stand for some hours until cold, then remove any fat from the top.

4. For a tomato soup completely free from pips it is advisable to sieve the tomatoes, or they can be skinned and deseeded.

5. Put the chopped tomatoes or the tomato purée into the pan with the clear stock, add the sprig of thyme, a bay leaf and a little extra seasoning if desired.

6. Many people like a slightly sweet taste to a tomato soup so a good pinch of sugar, preferably brown, can be added.

7. Cook until smooth then sieve if wished, to remove the thyme.

8. Serve with fresh rolls or bread.

Variation

For a thicker soup the tomatoes should be skinned and chopped and added to the stock with 2 diced potatoes, and 1 diced leek, then cooked until tender.

Clear celery soup

Cooking time: 2 hours
Preparation time: 20 minutes
Main cooking utensil: saucepan
Serves: 4–6

Imperial
carcass of a roasted chicken
3–4 pints water, use the
    smaller amount in a pressure
    cooker
1 head celery
2 onions
2 carrots
bouquet garni
2 bay leaves
seasoning
little jelly from the tin when
    roasting the chicken

Metric
carcass of a roasted chicken
$1\frac{3}{4}$–$2\frac{1}{4}$ litres water, use the
    smaller amount in a pressure
    cooker
1 head celery
2 onions
2 carrots
bouquet garni
2 bay leaves
seasoning
little jelly from the tin when
    roasting the chicken

1. Break the carcass into convenient-sized pieces, put them into a large saucepan, add the water, simmer for $1\frac{1}{2}$ hours or longer if wished; or put into a pressure cooker, cook at 15-lb. (7-kg.) pressure for 30 minutes, allow pressure to drop at room temperature (gradually).
2. Strain the stock carefully into a pan, add most of the celery stalks, saving the best part for garnish, the whole onions, carrots, bouquet garni, bay leaves and seasoning.
3. Simmer for 30 minutes or allow 10 minutes in a pressure cooker.
4. Strain again, re-heat with the jelly, the remaining chopped celery and extra seasoning. Serve topped with celery leaves.

Variation
Chicken broth: Make stock as above and add 2–3 stalks celery, 2 onions, 2 carrots, 1 leek, a small piece of turnip, all diced. Add the herbs and seasoning and the rice or barley and simmer for 45 minutes.

Clear soup with pancakes

Cooking time: 2¼ hours
Preparation time: 20 minutes
Main cooking utensils: saucepan, mixing bowl, small frying pan
Serves: 4–5

Imperial	Metric
chicken carcass or beef bones	chicken carcass or beef bones
2 pints water	generous litre water
2 onions	2 onions
2 carrots	2 carrots
2–3 teaspoons soup seasoning (see note)	2–3 teaspoons soup seasoning (see note)
Savoury pancake:	*Savoury pancake:*
2 oz. plain or self-raising flour	50 g. plain or self-raising flour
pinch salt	pinch salt
2 eggs	2 eggs
$\frac{1}{4}$ pint milk	125 ml. milk
pinch powdered nutmeg	pinch powdered nutmeg
$\frac{1}{2}$–1 teaspoon dried parsley	$\frac{1}{2}$–1 teaspoon dried parsley
butter	butter

1. Simmer the chicken carcass or the beef bones in the water with the onions and carrots for about 2 hours.

2. Strain the liquid into a saucepan, add the soup seasoning and simmer for about 10 minutes.

3. Meanwhile, make a savoury pancake by beating together the flour, salt, eggs, milk, nutmeg and dried parsley.

4. Heat some butter in a small frying pan and cook thin layers of the batter. Cut into strips and put on to the hot soup with a little chopped parsley.

Note: Soup seasoning is available from German delicatessens.

Variation

Turkish tripe soup: Blanch 1 lb. ($\frac{1}{2}$ kg.) tripe by putting the tripe into cold water, bringing it to the boil and discarding the water. This whitens the tripe. Now, simmer the tripe for 2–3 hours depending on the thickness, in 2 pints (generous litre) of salted water, together with a crushed clove of garlic and the juice of 1 lemon. Remove the meat from the liquid, mince or chop finely and return to the heat. Season well; an egg yolk may be blended with the liquid and cooked gently for a few minutes.

Cream of potato soup

Cooking time: 30 minutes
Preparation time: 25 minutes
Main cooking utensil: saucepan
Serves: 8–10

Imperial	Metric
1 lb. potatoes, peeled	½ kg. potatoes, peeled
1 pint chicken stock or water and 2 stock cubes	generous ½ litre chicken stock or water and 2 stock cubes
2 large onions	2 large onions
bay leaf	bay leaf
seasoning	seasoning
2 oz. butter	50 g. butter
2 oz. flour	50 g. flour
1 pint milk	500 ml. milk
½ pint thin cream	275 ml. thin cream
little cayenne pepper	little cayenne pepper
little celery salt	little celery salt
Garnish:	*Garnish:*
chopped parsley	chopped parsley

1. Put the potatoes — cut into small pieces — into the stock with the chopped onion, bay leaf and seasoning.
2. Cook until tender, do not boil too quickly.
3. Rub through a sieve.
4. Heat the butter in saucepan, stir in the flour, and cook for several minutes. Gradually stir in the milk, bring to the boil, cook until thick and smooth.
5. Add the potato purée and heat, then stir in the cream and seasoning, including the cayenne pepper and celery salt. Serve in individual soup cups or tureen, garnished with the parsley.

Variation

Make a potato leek soup with 10 oz. (300 g.) potatoes, 1 large onion, 12 oz. (300 g.) leeks, etc. Garnish with tiny croûtons of fried bread and paprika pepper and chopped watercress.

German potato soup

Cooking time: approximately 1 hour
Preparation time: 15 minutes
Main cooking utensil: large saucepan
Serves: 4

Imperial	Metric
6–8 oz. bacon (cut in one piece)	150 g. bacon (cut in one piece)
1 lb. old potatoes (weight when peeled)	$\frac{1}{2}$ kg. old potatoes (weight when peeled)
2 medium-sized leeks	2 medium-sized leeks
1 onion	1 onion
2$\frac{1}{2}$ pints water or stock	scant 1$\frac{1}{2}$ litres water or stock
1–2 teaspoons soup seasoning (see note)	1–2 teaspoons soup seasoning (see note)
3 white and 3 black peppercorns	3 white and 3 black peppercorns
4–5 pimento corns (see note)	4–5 pimento corns (see note)
2 bay leaves	2 bay leaves
pinch garlic salt	pinch garlic salt

1. Put the bacon, diced potatoes, finely chopped leeks and onion into a pan.

2. Add all the other ingredients and simmer gently until the vegetables are soft.

3. Remove the bacon, chop most of it finely, but save a few slices as a garnish. Return the bacon to the soup and heat.

4. Serve hot with rye bread, garnished with bacon.

Note: Available from German delicatessens.

Variation

Put 1 lb. ($\frac{1}{2}$ kg.) old potatoes, 2 leeks, 1 onion and 2 stalks celery (all prepared and chopped) into a pan with 2$\frac{1}{2}$ pints (1$\frac{1}{2}$ litres) stock, 2 sage leaves, a sprig of parsley and seasoning. Simmer until tender. Sieve the soup, add 2 oz. (50 g.) butter and reheat. Grill 2 oz. (50 g.) bacon and crumble. Sprinkle over the soup and serve with croûtons.

Liver dumpling soup

Cooking time: 5 minutes
Preparation time: 15 minutes plus 30 minutes standing
Main cooking utensil: saucepan
Serves: 4

Imperial	Metric
Dumplings:	*Dumplings:*
4 oz. calf's or lamb's or good quality ox liver	100 g. calf's or lamb's or good quality ox liver
1 small onion	1 small onion
seasoning	seasoning
pinch soup seasoning (see note)	pinch soup seasoning (see note)
2 oz. breadcrumbs	50 g. breadcrumbs
pinch marjoram	pinch marjoram
1 egg	1 egg
little milk	little milk
Soup:	*Soup:*
2 pints brown or white stock or water and stock cubes	generous litre brown or white stock or water and stock cubes
Garnish:	*Garnish:*
chopped parsley and/or chives	chopped parsley and/or chives

1. To make the dumplings, chop the liver finely or put it through a coarse mincer.

2. Chop or grate the onion, then blend with the liver, seasoning, breadcrumbs and herbs.

3. Press together very firmly, add the egg and enough milk to bind.

4. Leave this mixture to stand for 30 minutes, so that the breadcrumbs absorb the liquid.

5. Heat the stock, or water and stock cubes, then press the liver mixture through a coarse sieve into the boiling soup, or spoon into the liquid with a teaspoon.

6. Cook for a few minutes only.

7. Garnish with chopped parsley and/or chives.

Note: Soup seasoning is available from German delicatessens.

Variation

Czechoslovakian dumplings: Omit the onion and add 1 oz. (25 g.) extra breadcrumbs to the dumpling mixture. Blend in 1 oz. (25 g.) butter and a crushed clove of garlic if you like. Form the mixture into nut-sized dumplings and cook in the boiling stock for 5 minutes.

Kidney soup

Cooking time: lamb's kidneys 30 minutes, ox kidneys 1½ hours
Preparation time: 15 minutes
Main cooking utensil: large saucepan
Serves: 4–6

Imperial	**Metric**
8 oz. kidney (ox or lamb)	200 g. kidney (ox or lamb)
1 small onion	1 small onion
2 oz. butter	50 g. butter
1 oz. flour	25 g. flour
2 pints stock or water	generous litre stock or water
with 1–2 stock cubes	with 1–2 stock cubes
(see note)	(see note)
seasoning	seasoning
sprig of parsley	sprig of parsley
little port or Burgundy	little port or Burgundy

1. Chop the kidney very finely.
2. Fry with the finely chopped onion in hot butter for a minute or two. Be sure not to harden the outside of the meat.
3. Blend in the flour and gradually add the stock.
4. Bring to the boil, stir until smooth.
5. Simmer gently, adding seasoning and a sprig of parsley, for about 1½ hours.
6. To serve remove the parsley and add the port.

Note: With lamb's kidneys which need shorter cooking, use 1¼–1½ pints (¾ litre) only.

Variation
Oxtail soup: Soak one small chopped oxtail for 1–2 hours, discard the water. Fry 2 onions, 2 carrots and a little turnip at stage 2. Then continue as kidney soup.

Curried soup

Cooking time: 15 minutes
Preparation time: 15 minutes
Main cooking utensils: saucepan, electric blender or sieve
Serves: 4

Imperial	Metric
2 oz. butter	50 g. butter
2 large onions	2 large onions
1 pint chicken stock	generous $\frac{1}{2}$ litre chicken stock
1 level tablespoon curry powder	1 level tablespoon curry powder
1 level tablespoon cornflour	1 level tablespoon cornflour
water	water
2 egg yolks	2 egg yolks
$\frac{1}{4}$ pint cream	125 ml. cream
1 eating apple	1 eating apple
seasoning	seasoning
juice of $\frac{1}{2}$ lemon	juice of $\frac{1}{2}$ lemon
Garnish:	*Garnish:*
watercress	watercress
1–2 rashers bacon, grilled	1–2 rashers bacon, grilled

1. Melt the butter, add the chopped onions and cook until soft, but not brown.
2. Stir in the chicken stock and curry powder.
3. Add the cornflour mixed with a little water, bring to the boil and then simmer for 8 minutes.
4. Beat in the egg yolks into the cream and stir this mixture gradually into the hot soup.
5. Remove from the heat immediately and transfer mixture to electric blender with 1 apple, peeled, cored and sliced.
6. Blend until smooth, or press through a fine sieve – in this case the apple should be cooked with the soup before adding the egg yolks and cream.
7. Season to taste with salt, pepper and lemon juice. Either re-heat gently until hot, or chill and serve cold. Garnish with watercress and grilled chopped bacon.

Variation

Use beef instead of chicken stock. Garnish with tiny sprigs of raw cauliflower.

Consommé and garnishes

Cooking time: 1 hour
Preparation time: 20 minutes (including straining)
Main cooking utensil: large saucepan
Serves: 4

Imperial	Metric
12 oz. shin beef	300 g. shin beef
2 pints good brown stock	generous litre good brown stock
(see note)	(see note)
seasoning	seasoning
1 onion	1 onion
1 carrot	1 carrot
small piece celery	small piece celery
sprig parsley	sprig parsley
bay leaf	bay leaf

1. Cut the meat into neat pieces and put into the saucepan with the other ingredients.
2. Cover the pan tightly and simmer for 1 hour.
3. Strain through several thicknesses of muslin to give a clear liquid.
4. If the liquid is not clear, put in a whisked egg white and the clean shell.
5. Simmer for 20 minutes — any small particles of food collect on the shell and white.
6. Restrain carefully.
7. Heat the soup and add a little sherry or the garnishes given below.

Note: Make the stock from marrow bones.

Variations
Consommé julienne: Cut some carrot, turnip and cabbage into matchstick pieces, toss in butter and simmer in a little hot consommé until tender.
Consommé jardinière: As above but dice the vegetables.
With egg white: Hard-boil an egg and cut the white into fancy shapes — the yolk can also be used.
Jellied consommé: Dissolve 1–2 teaspoons powder gelatine in the hot consommé. Allow to set lightly, then whisk or chop and pile into soup cups.

41

Finnish fish soup

Cooking time: 30 minutes
Preparation time: 10 minutes
Main cooking utensil: saucepan
Serves: 4–6

Imperial	Metric
dried herbs	dried herbs
2½ pints water	scant 1½ litres water
2–3 oz. rice	50–75 g. rice
4 oz. green peas	100 g. green peas
seasoning	seasoning
8 oz. skinned, filleted fish	200 g. skinned, filleted fish
2 tablespoons concentrated tomato purée	2 tablespoons concentrated tomato purée
1 oz. cornflour	25 g. cornflour
¼ pint water	125 ml. water
good pinch salt	good pinch salt
paprika	paprika
garlic salt	garlic salt
Garnish:	*Garnish:*
parsley (optional)	parsley (optional)

1. Put dried herbs to taste into the water and add the rice, peas and seasoning.
2. Simmer for 15 minutes, then add the fish, cut into neat pieces, the tomato purée blended with the cornflour and the ¼ pint (125 ml.) water, salt, paprika and garlic salt.
3. Simmer for a further 10–15 minutes and garnish with parsley if wished.

Variation

Greek fish soup: Heat 2 tablespoons olive oil and toss 2 medium-sized chopped onions, 2 medium-sized chopped carrots and a crushed clove of garlic in it. Add 2½ pints (scant 1½ litres) water, rind of ½–1 lemon and seasoning and simmer for 30 minutes. Add 12 oz. (300 g.) skinned, dried fish, the juice of a lemon and a little chopped celery. Cook for a further 10 minutes. Lift out pieces of fish and strain the stock; put this back in the saucepan after blending it with 2 egg yolks and a little extra lemon juice if required. Thicken gently over a low heat without boiling, stirring constantly. Replace the fish and heat for a few minutes.

Bouillabaisse

Cooking time: 40 minutes
Preparation time: 30 minutes
Main cooking utensils: 2 saucepans
Serves: 8

Imperial	Metric
fish bones	fish bones
2½ pints water	scant 1½ litres water
seasoning	seasoning
1 strip orange peel	1 strip orange peel
bouquet garni	bouquet garni
3–4 tablespoons olive oil	3–4 tablespoons olive oil
5 medium-sized onions	5 medium-sized onions
4 cloves garlic	4 cloves garlic
1 tablespoon pimento	1 tablespoon pimento
6 peeled tomatoes	6 peeled tomatoes
¼ teaspoon nutmeg	¼ teaspoon nutmeg
2 lb. mixed filleted fish	1 kg. mixed filleted fish
2 pinches saffron	2 pinches saffron
1 tablespoon tomato purée	1 tablespoon tomato purée
¼ pint white wine	125 ml. white wine
few peeled prawns	few peeled prawns
chopped parsley	chopped parsley
To serve:	*To serve:*
croûtons or French bread	croûtons or French bread

1. Clean the fish bones and put into a pan with the water, seasoning, chopped orange peel and bouquet garni.
2. Boil rapidly until reduced to just less than 2 pints (1¼ litres).
3. Put the oil in another pan, add the finely sliced onions and chopped garlic.
4. Allow to brown. Add the chopped pimento, tomatoes and nutmeg, cook for a few minutes.
5. Increase the heat, add strained fish stock, chopped fish, saffron, tomato purée and wine.
6. Season to taste and simmer until the fish is well cooked but do not allow this to break.
7. Add the prawns and parsley immediately before serving. Serve with croûtons or French bread. This could be served as a main dish.

Variation

Any type of fish may be used provided it is free of bones. If liked, omit the white wine and add more stock in its place. Use less garlic.

White fish soup

Cooking time: 25–30 minutes
Preparation time: 20 minutes
Main cooking utensil: large saucepan
Serves: 8

Imperial	Metric
2 lb. cod	1 kg. cod
1 cod's head	1 cod's head
2 onions	2 onions
4 sticks celery	4 sticks celery
1 clove garlic (optional)	1 clove garlic (optional)
seasoning	seasoning
2 pints water	generous litre water
2 oz. flour	50 g. flour
$\frac{1}{2}$ pint milk	250 ml. milk
$\frac{1}{4}$ pint white wine	125 ml. white wine
2 tablespoons lemon juice	2 tablespoons lemon juice
4 oz. peeled prawns	100 g. peeled prawns
Garnish:	*Garnish:*
chopped parsley	chopped parsley

1. Put the fish, cod's head, chopped onions, celery and garlic into a large pan, season well and cover with the cold water.
2. Bring to the boil, simmer for 15—20 minutes until the fish is cooked.
3. Lift out the fish, strain stock and return to the pan.
4. Blend the flour with the milk, add the wine and mix well.
5. Stir into the fish stock and cook until thickened, stirring to keep the mixture smooth.
6. Flake half the cooked fish and add to the soup, simmer for 4—5 minutes.
7. Add the lemon juice to the soup, put in the prawns and remaining pieces of fish, heat for 1—2 minutes only.
8. Garnish with parsley. Serve very hot, with crisp toast.

Variation
Use a brown stock in place of the water and the milk.

Copenhagen consommé

Cooking time: 20 minutes
Preparation time: 15 minutes
Main cooking utensils: large saucepan, sieve
Serves: 6–8

Imperial	Metric
1 lb. firm white fish (hake, halibut or cod)	$\frac{1}{2}$ kg. firm white fish (hake, halibut or cod)
1 lb. fish bones	$\frac{1}{2}$ kg. fish bones
bouquet garni of parsley, celery and fennel	bouquet garni of parsley, celery and fennel
2 teaspoons salt	2 teaspoons salt
pepper	pepper
2 tablespoons lemon juice	2 tablespoons lemon juice
$\frac{1}{4}$ pint white wine	125 ml. white wine
$1\frac{1}{2}$ pints water	generous $\frac{3}{4}$ litre water
1 egg white (see note)	1 egg white (see note)
$\frac{3}{4}$ oz. gelatine	20 g. gelatine
1 leek	1 leek
2 sticks celery and 3 carrots cut into fine julienne shreds	2 sticks celery and 3 carrots cut into fine julienne shreds
lemon slices	lemon slices

1. Place the fish, fish bones, bouquet garni of herbs tied in muslin, salt, pinch pepper, lemon juice, wine and water in a large saucepan.
2. Bring to the boil and simmer covered for 15 minutes.
3. Strain through a fine sieve.
4. Whisk in the egg white and strain again.
5. Add the gelatine dissolved in a little water.
6. Taste and season again if necessary.
7. Leave to set lightly.
8. Cook julienne shreds for 3–4 minutes in fast boiling salted water. Drain and cool and add to the fish jelly. Leave to set.
9. When set, chop and pile in soup dishes, serve with lemon slices.

Note: An egg white is used to clear soups — any tiny particles that might spoil the clarity cling to this.

Variation
Use extra stock in place of white wine.

Summer fruit soup

Cooking time: 25–30 minutes
Preparation time: 15 minutes
Main cooking utensil: saucepan
Serves: 4–5

Imperial	Metric
1 lb. cooking apples or soft pears	$\frac{1}{2}$ kg. cooking apples or soft pears
2–3 fresh peaches or small can peaches (see note)	2–3 fresh peaches or small can peaches (see note)
1$\frac{1}{4}$ pints water	$\frac{3}{4}$ litre water
rind and juice of 2 lemons	rind and juice of 2 lemons
2 teaspoons cornflour	2 teaspoons cornflour
3–4 oz. sugar	75–100 g. sugar
1–2 teaspoons powdered cinnamon	1–2 teaspoons powdered cinnamon
Garnish:	*Garnish:*
lemon slice	lemon slice
watercress	watercress
To serve:	*To serve:*
$\frac{1}{4}$ pint soured or thick cream	125 ml. soured or thick cream

1. Peel, core and slice the apples or pears, remove the skin from the peaches but retain the stones, as these give a good flavour to the soup.
2. Put the fruit into a saucepan with the water and lemon rinds; be careful to use the top 'zest' of the lemon rinds only, so that the soup is not bitter.
3. Cook until the fruit is quite soft, then sieve and put into the saucepan.
4. Blend the cornflour with the lemon juice, stir into the soup, cook until thickened.
5. Add the sugar and cinnamon gradually, tasting as you do so, to make sure the mixture is refreshing with a certain 'bite'.
6. Chill thoroughly.
7. Serve garnished with lemon and watercress. The soured or whipped cream may be put on top of the soup or served separately.

Note: If using canned peaches, use the syrup instead of some of the water and use a little less sugar. You can omit the peaches and use extra apples or pears instead.

Variation
Use white wine in place of some of the water. Instead of apples or pears, use sour (Morello) cherries; cherry or ordinary plums; or half damsons and half apples.

Lemon soup

Cooking time: 1 hour
Preparation time: 15 minutes
Main cooking utensil: saucepan
Serves: 4–5

Imperial

2 pints water or half water and half apple juice or half water and half wine
3 oz. sago (see note)
3 lemons
2 egg yolks
½–1 oz. vanilla sugar
pinch powdered ginger
sugar to taste
Topping:
2 egg whites
½–1 oz. sugar
little powdered cinnamon
a few ratafia biscuits (tiny macaroons)

Metric

generous 1 litre water or half water and half apple juice or half water and half wine
75 g. sago (see note)
3 lemons
2 egg yolks
15–25 g. vanilla sugar
pinch powdered ginger
sugar to taste
Topping:
2 egg whites
15–25 g. sugar
little powdered cinnamon
a few ratafia biscuits (tiny macaroons)

1. Bring the water, or apple juice and water or wine and water to the boil.

2. Put in the sago and stir for a few minutes to prevent it dropping to the bottom of the pan.

3. Lower the heat, add the rind of 1–2 lemons and simmer the sago until quite clear. The soup can be sieved, then re-heated if wished.

4. Blend the lemon juice with the egg yolks, add to the soup together with the vanilla sugar and powdered ginger.

5. Simmer gently until slightly thickened by the egg yolks, but do not allow to boil.

6. Taste the soup and add sugar as required, do not make this too sweet for it should be refreshing on a hot day. Chill thoroughly.

7. Pour into the serving dish or dishes.

8. Whisk the egg whites until very stiff, drop in spoonfuls on soup, top with sugar and 'bands' of powdered cinnamon. Serve at once, with ratafias.

Note: If people dislike the look of sago, use rice instead, or sieve as suggested. This is a delicious sweet soup, ideal for summer.

Variation

Omit meringue and ratafias.

American dips

There are excellent dehydrated foods that can be used to give the flavour needed for dips and below are some examples of how these can be used, together with alternatives if they are not available.

Caesar dip

Mix together 4 oz. (100 g.) cottage cheese and 5 oz. (125 ml.) soured cream or use thin cream with $\frac{1}{2}$ tablespoon lemon juice. Stir in a complete packet of Caesar dip, leave for 1 hour. Meanwhile fry 2–3 rashers bacon until crisp, add some of the cool, chopped bacon to the dip. Put the mixture into the bowl, top with the rest of the bacon. (1 oz. (25 g.) crisp crumbs and 4 oz. (100 g.) grated cheese can be used instead of the Caesar dip.)

Creamy horseradish dip

Mix a complete packet of horseradish dip with $\frac{1}{2}$ pint (250 ml.) soured cream or use thin cream and a good tablespoon lemon juice. Chill for 1 hour then add $\frac{1}{2}$ finely diced green and $\frac{1}{2}$ finely diced red pepper. Put into the bowl and top with more chopped pepper. (Use horseradish cream instead of the dip.)

Toasted onion dip

Mix together 4 oz. (150 g.) cottage cheese and 4 oz. (100 g.) soured cream or use thin cream with $\frac{1}{2}$ tablespoon lemon juice. Stir in a complete packet of toasted onion dip. Leave for at least an hour in a cool place. Put into a bowl and top with rings of fried onion. (To replace the dip, chop and fry 2 medium-sized onions until golden brown; chop again to make sure they are very fine and add to the other ingredients.)

Green onion dip

Mix 8 oz. (225 g.) cottage cheese with 2 tablespoons soured cream or thin cream and a good squeeze lemon juice. Stir in a complete packet of green onion dip. Leave in a cool place for an hour. Put into a bowl and top with chopped chives or spring onions. (Use finely crushed spring onion tops or chives when no dip is available.)

Note: To serve, dip cubes of ham, fried bread, olives or potato crisps.

Cheese and paprika dip and Blue cheese and onion dip

Preparation time: 10 minutes
Main utensil: mixing bowl
Serves: 4

Cheese and paprika dip

Imperial
6 oz. cream cheese
2 oz. margarine
2 tablespoons chopped parsley
2 tablespoons chives
$\frac{1}{2}$ tablespoon milk or thin cream
seasoning
1–2 teaspoons paprika pepper
Garnish:
chopped chives
spring onions or parsley

Metric
150 g. cream cheese
50 g. margarine
2 tablespoons chopped parsley
2 tablespoons chives
$\frac{1}{2}$ tablespoon milk or thin cream
seasoning
1–2 teaspoons paprika pepper
Garnish:
chopped chives
spring onions or parsley

1. Blend the cream cheese and margarine.
2. Gradually add the other ingredients, adding seasoning and paprika to taste.
3. Put into a cold place, this dip is best if left overnight for the flavours to infuse. Cover to prevent the top drying.
4. Put into a shallow bowl, arrange biscuits, crisps or vegetables around. Top with chives, spring onion or parsley.

Blue cheese and onion dip

Imperial
6 oz. Danish blue cheese
2 oz. margarine
2 tablespoons chopped parsley
3 tablespoons soured cream or
   fresh thin cream and a
   squeeze of lemon juice
1 small onion
salt
freshly ground black pepper
Garnish:
chopped chives
spring onions or parsley

Metric
150 g. Danish blue cheese
50 g. margarine
2 tablespoons chopped parsley
3 tablespoons soured cream or
   fresh thin cream and a
   squeeze of lemon juice
1 small onion
salt
freshly ground black pepper
Garnish:
chopped chives
spring onions or parsley

1. Crumble the cheese, then blend with the margarine and cream well.
2. Add the rest of the ingredients, chopping the onion very finely or better still, grating it.
3. Season well and put into a cold place, see stage 3 above.
4. Serve in a bowl with vegetables, etc., as above.

Cauliflower and piquant sauce dip

Preparation time: 10 minutes
Main utensil: large bowl
Serves: 4

Imperial	Metric
1 small cauliflower (see note)	1 small cauliflower (see note)
salt	salt
celery salt	celery salt
paprika pepper (optional)	paprika pepper (optional)
Sauce:	*Sauce:*
just over $\frac{1}{4}$ pint mayonnaise	just over 150 ml. mayonnaise
$\frac{1}{4}$ pint tomato ketchup	125 ml. tomato ketchup
1 tablespoon lemon juice	1 tablespoon lemon juice
shake cayenne pepper	shake cayenne pepper
4 tablespoons thick cream	4 tablespoons thick cream
2 tablespoons sherry or white wine	2 tablespoons sherry or white wine
few drops Worcestershire sauce	few drops Worcestershire sauce

1. Wash the cauliflower, divide into neat flowerets (discarding the thick pieces of stalk).
2. Arrange around the edge of a large dish, season lightly with salt, celery salt and paprika pepper.
3. Blend the ingredients for the sauce together, tasting as you do so, for it should have a sharp piquant flavour.
4. Put the sauce into a shallow bowl in the centre of the cauliflower.
5. Dip pieces of cauliflower into the sauce.

Note: Cauliflower must be very fresh to avoid an over-strong flavour.

Variation

Cauliflower cheese dip: Wash the cauliflower, pull away the flowerets, chop most of these very finely with a few chives to get a good blending of flavours.

Add 4 tablespoons mayonnaise, 12 oz. (300 g.) grated Cheddar cheese, $\frac{1}{4}$ pint (125 ml.) thick cream, 2 tablespoons lemon juice, a few drops of Worcestershire sauce and seasoning. Blend well and if necessary add a little extra liquid to give a soft consistency. Put into a shallow bowl on a large plate, surround with the rest of the cauliflower, cheese biscuits and crisps.

Hot cheese savouries

Cooking time: see method
Preparation time: for 3 recipes 50 minutes
Main cooking utensils: 2 baking trays, frying pan, ovenproof dish
Oven temperature: hot (450–475°F., 230–240°C., Gas Mark 8–9)
Oven position: see methods
Makes: about 3½ dozen savouries

Cheese puffs

Imperial
8 oz. frozen puff pastry
2 oz. grated Parmesan cheese
1 egg white

Metric
200 g. frozen puff pastry
50 g. grated Parmesan cheese
1 egg white

1. Roll out the pastry until paper thin.
2. Sprinkle with most of the cheese, fold in three, roll out again until $\frac{1}{8}$ inch ($\frac{1}{4}$ cm.) thick.
3. Cut into $\frac{1}{2}$-inch (1-cm.) strips about 3 inches ($7\frac{1}{2}$ cm.) in length, brush with egg white, top with the rest of the cheese.
4. Bake for about 12 minutes above the centre of the hot oven.

Cheese rolls

Imperial
9 large wafer-thin slices bread
3 oz. cream cheese
1 oz. grated Parmesan cheese
seasoning
1 tablespoon chopped chives
little butter

Metric
9 large wafer-thin slices bread
75 g. cream cheese
25 g. grated Parmesan cheese
seasoning
1 tablespoon chopped chives
little butter

1. Halve the slices of bread, remove the crusts.
2. Mix the cream and grated cheeses, add the seasoning and chives, spread over the bread. Roll, secure with cocktail sticks.
3. Brush with melted butter, bake for 2–3 minutes in the centre of the hot oven.

Mushroom croûtes

Imperial
18 small rounds bread
3 oz. butter
18 mushrooms
4 oz. cream cheese

Metric
18 small rounds bread
75 g. butter
18 mushrooms
100 g. cream cheese

1. Fry the bread in half the butter, drain well, put on the ovenproof dish. Fry the mushroom caps and stalks in the rest of the butter, put the caps on the bread and fill with cheese.
2. Put the stalks in the centre, heat for few minutes in oven.

Cheese appetisers

German households serve delicious snacks with cocktails or coffee, and the picture shows some of the easiest and most pleasant ones. Choose either German cheese (Limburger is very strong, Tilsiter has excellent flavour, or German Camembert), or cream cheese, but other cheeses may also be used.

Fruit and cheese
Cut shapes in a firm, fairly strong-flavoured cheese, put on to cocktail sticks with glacé cherries, or mandarin oranges.

Ribbon sandwiches
For each person, butter 4 slices rye bread and make 3-layer sandwiches. Layer (a) soft curd cheese blended with paprika pepper and a little tomato purée or ketchup; layer (b) a slice of Camembert cheese; layer (c) blend soft cream cheese with plenty of chopped parsley, finely chopped dill, chopped chives, and thick cream to moisten. Leave the sandwiches in a cool place with a board on top to weight them down, then after an hour or two cut into narrow ribbon shapes, turn on their sides.

Camembert triangles
Cut triangles of ripe (but not over-ripe) Camembert cheese and top with pieces of gherkin or pickled cucumber. Put on to cocktail sticks. Also cut neat slices of cheese, then cut into small fingers and pile high as shown in the pictures.

Käseschnitten
These hot Austrian cheese slices are often served with a clear soup, but they make an excellent appetiser. Make a thick sauce of 1 oz. (25 g.) butter, 1 oz. (25 g.) flour, $\frac{1}{4}$ pint (125 ml.) milk, seasoning. Blend in 1 oz. (25 g.) grated Parmesan, 2 oz. (25 g.) grated Edam, 1 oz. (25 g.) grated Cheddar, a few caraway seeds, and paprika to taste. Halve the tiny rolls, butter, top with the cheese mixture, sprinkle with cheese, heat in the oven and serve at once.

Cheese balls
Roll cream cheese into balls, then into ground, browned nuts or crisp crumbs, and put on to cocktail sticks.

Canapés and open sandwiches

Cocktail snacks

Spear the following with cocktail sticks:

1. Emmenthal in fancy shapes (cut with a pastry cutter), dipped in paprika, topped with a slice of gherkin and a pearl onion.
2. Sliver of red pepper wrapped around the top of a piece of Gruyère and then a pearl onion.
3. Gruyère with a stuffed olive.
4. Layers of Sbrinz (see note), each spread with herb butter (see note) or herby cottage cheese, and topped with a rosette of herb butter.
5. Gruyère with a piece of pineapple dipped in curry powder.
6. Gruyère with a black olive.
7. Slices of Gruyère with slices of pimento topped with a gherkin slice.
8. Emmenthal with a slice of candied lime or orange peel.
9. Slices of Gruyère with slices of gherkin, topped with a rolled anchovy.
10. Gruyère with a slice of preserved apricot.
11. Gruyère with a slice of mushroom.
12. Gruyère with a preserved or maraschino cherry.

Open cheese sandwiches

Spread butter on thinly sliced bread and add a thin layer of mustard or mayonnaise. Cover with slices of Emmenthal or Gruyère cheese, cut to the shape of the bread. Garnish with tomatoes, slices of hard-boiled egg, gherkins and olives.

Cheese-butter canapés

Blend equal quantities of butter and grated Swiss cheese (see note), season and spread, or pipe on $\frac{1}{4}$-inch ($\frac{1}{2}$-cm.) thick slices of bread.

Note: You can put cheese spread into three bowls and vary the basic flavour with chopped herbs, tomato purée or caraway seeds. Sbrinz is a hard cheese, if unobtainable, use Parmesan. For herb butter, blend chopped herbs with butter.

Prawn eggs

Cooking time: 10 minutes
Preparation time: 15 minutes
Main cooking utensil: saucepan
Serves: 2–4

Imperial	Metric
4 eggs	4 eggs
1 oz. butter	25 g. butter
1 tablespoon cream or	1 tablespoon cream or
mayonnaise (see below)	mayonnaise (see below)
2–3 oz. small prawns	50–75 g. small prawns
seasoning	seasoning
Garnish:	*Garnish:*
lettuce	lettuce
8 prawns	8 prawns
parsley or chives	parsley or chives

1. Boil the eggs for 10 minutes until hard-boiled, plunge immediately into cold water to prevent a dark line forming round the yolks.
2. Shell before they get cold, halve and carefully spoon the yolks into a basin.
3. Mash with a fork (if you let the eggs get too cold, this is much more difficult to do).
4. Add the butter, the cream, and most of the prawns which should be finely chopped, but leave 8 for garnish.
5. Season and pile back into the white cases. Serve on a bed of crisp lettuce garnished with prawns, parsley or chives.

For the mayonnaise: Blend an egg yolk with a pinch of salt, pepper, mustard and sugar, add a tablespoon of vinegar or lemon juice, then gradually blend in oil, drop by drop, beating well with wooden spoon to give a smooth sauce. 1 egg yolk takes from $\frac{1}{4}-\frac{1}{2}$ pint (150–250 ml.) of oil, but a less oily dressing can be made.

Variations

Use grated cheese or finely chopped ham or chicken or mashed sardines in place of prawns, or simply flavour the egg with mayonnaise or with curry powder and chutney.

Melon cocktail

Preparation time: 10 minutes
Main utensils: vegetable scoop, basin
Serves: 4

Imperial	**Metric**
ripe firm melon, either canteloup or charentais	1 ripe firm melon, either canteloup or charentais
1-1½ tablespoons honey	1-1½ tablespoons honey
Liqueur to flavour:	*Liqueur to flavour:*
Kirsch, Cointreau, Maraschino or use a wine like dry sherry or champagne	Kirsch, Cointreau, Maraschino or use a wine like dry sherry or champagne
Decoration:	*Decoration:*
mint	mint

1. Either halve the melon or cut a slice from the top.
2. Remove all the seeds, then cut the flesh into balls with the vegetable scoop. This is not difficult to do, but it needs practice — insert the scoop into the flesh, then gradually turn it, so it cuts into the flesh and forms a ball.
3. Remove carefully, so the flesh is not broken in any way.
4. Put the balls into the basin with the honey and the liqueur or wine to give a good flavour.
5. Any small 'untidy' pieces of melon could be saved to use in a fruit salad or fruit cocktail (see below).
6. Chill the cocktail before serving.
7. Put either into sundae or tall glasses and top with sprigs of mint.

Jellied melon basket

Preparation time: 20 minutes
Main cooking utensil: saucepan
Serves: 6–8

Imperial	**Metric**
juice of 2 lemons	juice of 2 lemons
juice of 2 oranges	juice of 2 oranges
water	water
$\frac{1}{2}$ oz. gelatine	15 g. gelatine
sugar to taste	sugar to taste
1 melon	1 melon
1 dessert pear	1 dessert pear
Decoration:	*Decoration:*
glacé cherries	glacé charries

1. Make 2 cuts at top of the melon about $1-1\frac{1}{2}$ inches (2–3 cm.) apart. Continue to the centre of the melon. This is the basis of the handle. Cut into the flesh round the centre of the melon, remove 2 portions, cut away the pulp from under the 'handle' and base of the melon.

2. Measure the fruit juices. Add enough water to give barely 1 pint (550 ml.).

3. Soften the gelatine in a little of this liquid, and dissolve in a basin over hot water, add sugar to taste.

4. Mix with the rest of the water and allow to cool and begin to thicken slightly.

5. When the jelly begins to stiffen, add the diced melon pulp and the neatly diced pear and put back into the melon case.

6. When set lightly, decorate with glacé cherries.

Variation

Serve this as a sweet instead of an hors d'oeuvre. Increase the sugar to 2–3 oz.

Eggs in tomato jelly

Cooking time: 10 minutes
Preparation time: 15 minutes, plus time for jelly to set
Main cooking utensils: 2 saucepans, 8 small individual moulds
Serves: 8

Imperial	Metric
½ oz. (1 envelope) powdered gelatine	15 g. (1 envelope) powdered gelatine
2 tablespoons lemon juice	2 tablespoons lemon juice
1 pint tomato juice less 4 tablespoons	500 ml. tomato juice
2 tablespoons dry sherry	2 tablespoons dry sherry
few drops Tabasco sauce	few drops Tabasco sauce
few drops Worcestershire sauce	few drops Worcestershire sauce
seasoning	seasoning
8 eggs	8 eggs
1 medium-sized can asparagus tips	1 medium-sized can asparagus tips
lettuce	lettuce
¼ cucumber	¼ cucumber

1. Soften the gelatine in the lemon juice.
2. Heat the tomato juice, add the softened gelatine and stir until dissolved.
3. Stir in the sherry, Tabasco sauce and Worcestershire sauce, season well.
4. Allow to cool, but not set.
5. Meanwhile cook the eggs until just hard-boiled, crack the shells, put the eggs into cold water then shell.
6. Put a little cool tomato mixture into each mould with 2–3 asparagus tips.
7. Allow to set, then add an egg to each mould and cover with the tomato liquid.
8. Allow to set then turn out on to a bed of lettuce.
9. Garnish with asparagus tips and sliced cucumber. Serve as an hors d'oeuvre or for a buffet party.

Note: This is an ideal dish to make beforehand and keep in the refrigerator.

Variations
Use aspic jelly in place of tomato juice. Use all tomato juice and omit lemon juice and sherry.

Pickled herrings

Cooking time: 8 minutes
Preparation time: 20 minutes, plus time to stand (see note and
  stages 1 and 6)
Main cooking utensil: saucepan
Serves: 4

Imperial	Metric
4 large salt or fresh herrings (see stage 1)	4 large salt or fresh herrings (see stage 1)
$\frac{1}{2}$ pint brown or white vinegar	275 ml. brown or white vinegar
$\frac{1}{2}$ pint water	275 ml. water
2–4 oz. sugar (see note)	50–100 g. sugar (see note)
2 teaspoons pickling spice	2 teaspoons pickling spice
2 bay leaves	2 bay leaves
bunch fresh dill or pinch dried dill	bunch fresh dill or pinch dried dill
2 carrots	2 carrots
1 turnip	1 turnip
2 onions	2 onions
2 leeks	2 leeks
stick celery	stick celery
seasoning	seasoning
Garnish:	*Garnish:*
red and green chilli peppers (optional)	red and green chilli peppers (optional)
1 medium-sized onion	1 medium-sized onion
2 lemons	2 lemons
2 firm tomatoes	2 firm tomatoes

1. If using salt herrings, cover with cold water and stand overnight. If using fresh herrings (as in picture) clean, divide into 2 fillets and do not soak; use at once.

2. Divide the salt fish into small pieces.

3. Put the vinegar, water, sugar and pickling spices into a pan, simmer steadily for 8 minutes, making sure the sugar is dissolved.

4. Put the herrings, bay leaves, dill and diced vegetables into a dish, cover with the hot pickling mixture.

5. Add seasoning to taste, fresh fish should be well salted.

6. Wait until liquid is no longer steaming, then put into a cool place, preferably a refrigerator. Fresh herrings should be stored for 1–2 days only if no refrigerator is available. Serve with the vegetables and garnish.

Note: Salt herrings are obtainable from many fishmongers, but fresh may be used. Other fish to treat in this way are mackerel and whiting. Swedish pickled herrings are often very sweet, so the amount of sugar depends on personal taste. Serve this dish when herrings are in season and cheap.

Stuffed ham salad

Preparation time: 12 minutes
Main utensils: mixing bowls
Serves: 6

Imperial	Metric
6 large or 12 smaller slices cooked ham (see note)	6 large or 12 smaller slices cooked ham (see note)
Filling:	*Filling:*
4 oz. raw mushrooms	100 g. raw mushrooms
1 green pepper	1 green pepper
1 clove garlic	1 clove garlic
grated rind and juice of 1 lemon	grated rind and juice of 1 lemon
2 large tomatoes	2 large tomatoes
2 tablespoons mayonnaise	2 tablespoons mayonnaise
seasoning	seasoning
Salad:	*Salad:*
1 red or green pepper	1 red or green pepper
cucumber	cucumber
2 tomatoes	2 tomatoes
1 lettuce	1 lettuce
3 tablespoons olive oil	3 tablespoons olive oil
1–2 teaspoon French mustard	1–2 teaspoons French mustard
seasoning	seasoning
1½ tablespoons lemon juice	1½ tablespoons lemon juice
Garnish:	*Garnish:*
¼ cucumber	¼ cucumber
2 lemons	2 lemons
parsley	parsley

1. If using large slices of ham, cut in half to make smaller slices.
2. Slice the mushrooms and the flesh from the green pepper, discarding the core and seeds.
3. Crush the garlic, blend with the lemon rind and juice, mushrooms and chopped pepper.
4. Skin and chop the tomatoes, add to the other ingredients, bind with mayonnaise and season.
5. Put this soft filling on to each slice of ham, roll firmly.
6. Slice pepper, cucumber and tomatoes; shred lettuce.
7. Blend the oil with the mustard, seasoning and lemon juice, toss the salad in most of this, and put into a bowl.
8. Top with the ham rolls, then garnish with the cucumber slices dipped in the remaining oil and lemon juice, sliced lemon, strips of lemon zest and parsley. Serve as an hors d'oeuvre or as a light main dish.

Note: Italian smoked Parma ham could be used.

Variation

Use only 2 oz. (50 g.) mushrooms, omit the pepper and use 4 oz. (100 g.) soft cream cheese (Italian ricotta is ideal) in the filling.

Mushroom and ham tart

Cooking time: 55 minutes
Preparation time: 25 minutes
Main cooking utensils: 7-inch (18-cm.) cake tin, preferably with
   loose base, frying pan
Oven temperature: moderately hot (400°F., 200°C., Gas Mark 6)
Oven position: centre
Serves: 8

Imperial	Metric
Pastry:	Pastry:
10 oz. flour, preferably plain	250 g. flour, preferably plain
pinch salt	pinch salt
5 oz. butter	125 g. butter
water to mix	water to mix
Filling:	Filling:
1 large onion	1 large onion
1 clove garlic	1 clove garlic
2 oz. butter	50 g. butter
1 oz. flour	25 g. flour
¼ pint brown stock	125 ml. brown stock
½ lb. mushrooms	¾ kg. mushrooms
10–12 oz. cooked ham	250–300 g. cooked ham
2 eggs	2 eggs
seasoning	seasoning
Garnish:	Garnish:
parsley	parsley

1. Sieve the flour and salt, rub in the butter until the mixture resembles fine breadcrumbs, then bind with water.

2. Roll out the pastry to a large round, put into the tin. Do not trim away edges, the pastry round should be large enough to line the tin and leave a border at the top.

3. Chop the onion, crush the garlic, fry in hot butter for 5–10 minutes, taking care the onion does not brown.

4. Blend the flour with the stock, pour into the pan. Stir over a low heat until the mixture thickens.

5. Chop the mushrooms and ham, add the onion mixture and cool. Stir in the beaten eggs and season well.

6. Put the mixture into the pastry-lined tin; fold the edges of the pastry over the filling and neaten, mark with a fork.

7. Bake for approximately 45 minutes; lower the heat slightly if the tart seems to be over-cooking.

8. Garnish with parsley. This could also be served with salad as a light main dish.

Note: Use mushroom stalks for greater economy.

Salmon mousse

Cooking time: few minutes
Preparation time: 15 minutes plus setting time
Main cooking utensils: 4 ½-pint (¼-litre) individual moulds or
    6 smaller moulds, saucepan
Serves: 4–6

Imperial	Metric
1-pint packet aspic jelly	$\frac{1}{2}$-litre packet aspic jelly
approximately 1 pint hot water	approximately $\frac{1}{2}$ litre hot water
or well strained fish stock	or well strained fish stock
made with skin and bones of	made with skin and bones of
fish	fish
little oil	little oil
few tarragon leaves	few tarragon leaves
2–3 gherkins	2–3 gherkins
1–2 cooked carrots	1–2 cooked carrots
2 level teaspoons powdered	2 level teaspoons powdered
gelatine	gelatine
2 tablespoons dry sherry	2 tablespoons dry sherry
1 lb. cooked or canned salmon	$\frac{1}{2}$ kg. cooked or canned salmon
3 tablespoons mayonnaise	3 tablespoons mayonnaise
grated rind and juice of $\frac{1}{2}$ lemon	grated rind and juice of $\frac{1}{2}$ lemon
seasoning	seasoning
2 egg whites	2 egg whites
Garnish:	*Garnish:*
1 lemon	1 lemon
2 tomatoes	2 tomatoes
lettuce	lettuce

1. Dissolve the aspic jelly in the hot water or stock (see note).
2. Allow to cool then spoon a little into each oiled mould (use approximately a third of the jelly).
3. As the jelly thickens turn it in the mould so that it coats the bottom and sides.
4. Arrange individual tarragon leaves, pieces of gherkin and carrot on the jelly.
5. Carefully spoon a very thin layer of cool but liquid jelly over the garnish. Allow to set.
6. Re-heat the remaining aspic, add the gelatine, softened in sherry, stir until dissolved. Cool and allow to stiffen slightly.
7. Add the flaked salmon, mayonnaise, grated lemon rind and juice, seasoning, and finally the stiffly beaten egg whites.
8. Spoon into the moulds, allow to set. Turn out and garnish. Serve as an hors d'oeuvre or light fish course.

Note: See packet for exact amount of liquid to use.

Variation
Cooked white fish or shellfish (crab in particular) can be used.

Apple and tomato moulds

Cooking time: few minutes to dissolve gelatine
Preparation time: 10 minutes
Main cooking utensils: saucepan, 4 moulds
Serves: 4

Imperial	Metric
¾ pint tomato juice	425 ml. tomato juice
½ oz. gelatine	15 g. gelatine
¼ pint water	150 ml. water
1 tablespoon Worcestershire sauce	1 tablespoon Worcestershire sauce
½ teaspoon salt	½ teaspoon salt
¼ teaspoon pepper	¼ teaspoon pepper
1 apple	1 apple
2 oz. ham, chopped	50 g. ham, chopped
Garnish:	*Garnish:*
few lettuce leaves	few lettuce leaves

1. Pour the tomato juice into a bowl.
2. Soak the gelatine in the water for 5 minutes and dissolve over a gentle heat (see note).
3. Add to the tomato juice and stir well.
4. Add the Worcestershire sauce and seasoning and stir well until the mixture begins to thicken.
5. Peal and core the apple. Chop the apple and ham neatly and add to the mixture. Pour into the four moulds.
6. Leave to set firmly.
7. When set, turn on to a bed of lettuce.

Note: Gelatine dissolves more readily if soaked in cold liquid for a short time – it should not be boiled. With small quantities of liquid, dissolve in a basin over hot water – otherwise in a saucepan over a very low heat.

Variation
Use grated cheese instead of ham.

Ham mousse

Cooking time: few minutes
Preparation time: 20 minutes
Main cooking utensils: basin, saucepan, 7- to 8-inch (18- to 20-cm.)
  ring tin
Serves: 5–6

Imperial	Metric
1 lb. canned or cooked ham	$\frac{1}{2}$ kg. canned or cooked ham
3 tablespoons thick cream	6 tablespoons thick cream
3 tablespoons thin cream	3 tablespoons thin cream
1 level tablespoon powdered gelatine	1 level tablespoon powdered gelatine
2 tablespoons water	2 tablespoons water
$\frac{1}{2}$–1 teaspoon made mustard	$\frac{1}{2}$–1 teaspoon made mustard
1–2 egg whites (see stage 4)	1–2 egg whites (see stage 4)
seasoning (see stage 5)	seasoning (see stage 5)
Garnish:	Garnish:
parsley	parsley
lettuce	lettuce
tomato	tomato
cucumber	cucumber

1. Chop the ham finely, blend any fat with lean (canned ham tends to be almost entirely lean).
2. Put the thick cream into a basin, whip until it begins to thicken, add the thin cream, continue whipping until the mixture holds its shape; this gives the excellent light cream so popular in Denmark, where this recipe comes from.
3. Put the gelatine and cold water into a basin, stand over a pan of boiling water, heat until dissolved, then add to the chopped ham, fold the cream into the gelatine mixture with the mustard.
4. Whisk the egg whites or white until very stiff, naturally 2 egg whites make a lighter mixture.
5. Fold into the ham mixture, taste and season carefully, a good shake of pepper is necessary, but the amount of salt will depend upon the ham. Danish ham is generally very mild.
6. Spoon into the prepared mould, leave until set then turn out. Garnish with parsley, lettuce, tomato and cucumber. Serve with toast.

Note: To prepare mould for a savoury jelly, brush lightly with olive oil, this makes the jelly turn out easily.

Stuffed pork pâté

Cooking time: 2 hours
Preparation time: 25 minutes plus overnight soaking of prunes
Main cooking utensils: 2 saucepans, 1½- to 2-lb. (¾- to 1-kg.) loaf
  tin, ovenproof plate
Oven temperature: moderate (350–375°F., 180–190°C.,
  Gas Mark 4–5)
Oven position: centre
Serves: 8

Imperial	Metric
4 oz. dried prunes	100 g. dried prunes
2 medium-sized cooking apples	2 medium-sized cooking apples
pinch chopped sage	pinch chopped sage
Pâté:	*Pâté:*
3 eggs	3 eggs
1½ lb. lean pork	¾ kg. lean pork
4 oz. soft breadcrumbs	100 g. soft breadcrumbs
¼ pint milk	125 ml. milk
1–2 tablespoons chopped chives or spring onions	1–2 tablespoons chopped chives or spring onions
½ lemon	½ lemon
seasoning	seasoning
Topping:	*Topping:*
4–6 oz. grated Gruyère or Cheddar cheese	100–150 g. grated Gruyère or Cheddar cheese
2–3 tablespoons thick cream	2–3 tablespoons thick cream

1. Soak the prunes overnight or for some hours in cold water, simmer until tender, save a few for garnish.
2. Stone the remainder of the prunes. Peel and quarter the apples, sprinkle with sage.
3. Hard-boil 2 eggs, crack and shell.
4. Mince the pork, blend with the chopped hard-boiled eggs, raw egg, breadcrumbs (soaked in milk and beaten until smooth), chives and grated lemon rind and juice to taste. Season well.
5. Put half the mixture into a greased tin, spoon the prune and apple mixture down the centre, then top with the remainder of the pork pâté.
6. Cover with greased foil or paper and bake for 1¼ hours.
7. Turn out of the tin, put on an ovenproof plate, blend the cheese and cream, spread over the top of loaf and heat under the grill or in the oven until the cheese has melted.
8. Serve as a hot or cold pâté, topped with prunes. If serving cold, the cheese could be blended with mayonnaise instead of cream.

Coral island eggs

Cooking time: few minutes plus time to hard-boil eggs
Preparation time: 15 minutes
Main cooking utensils: saucepan, frying pan
Serves: 8

Imperial	Metric
8 oz. peeled shrimps	200 g. peeled shrimps
2 oz. butter or pork fat	50 g. butter or pork fat
2 egg whites	2 egg whites
2 teaspoons Chinese (Shao Shing) wine or sherry	2 teaspoons Chinese (Shao Shing) wine or sherry
2 teaspoons ginger juice from preserved ginger	2 teaspoons ginger juice from preserved ginger
seasoning	seasoning
8 thick slices white bread	8 thick slices white bread
4 hard-boiled eggs	4 hard-boiled eggs
fat for deep-frying	fat for deep-frying
Garnish:	*Garnish:*
parsley	parsley

1. Finely chop the shrimps and mix well with the butter.
2. Add 1 egg white and mix in the sherry, ginger juice and seasoning.
3. Cut the bread into diamond shapes, place a small mound of the mixture on each piece.
4. Halve the hard-boiled eggs lengthwise, place one half, flat side down on each mound, pressing the mixture firmly round the base.
5. Brush all over with the second egg white.
6. Fry in the deep fat, egg side downwards, turn over and continue cooking until the bread is golden brown.
7. Remove from the fat, drain on absorbent paper. Serve at once, garnished with parsley.

Note: These must be eaten fresh after frying, but could be served cold.

Variation

If no ginger juice is available, use the syrup from a tin of pineapple, with a pinch of ginger powder.

Salmon loaf with cream sauce

Cooking time: 1¼ hours
Preparation time: 25 minutes
Main cooking utensils: saucepan, 1½- to 2-lb. (¾- to 1-kg.) loaf tin, frying pan
Oven temperature: very moderate (325–350°F., 170–180°C., Gas Mark 3–4)
Oven position: centre
Serves: 10

Imperial	Metric
$\frac{3}{4}$–1 lb. salmon or salmon trout or canned salmon	$\frac{1}{4}$–$\frac{1}{2}$ kg. salmon or salmon trout or canned salmon
1 lb. white fish, weight without skin and bones	$\frac{1}{2}$ kg. white fish, weight without skin and bones
few prawns	few prawns
2 oz. butter	50 g. butter
2 oz. flour	50 g. flour
$\frac{1}{2}$ pint milk	250 ml. milk
2 eggs	2 eggs
3 teaspoons chopped parsley	3 teaspoons chopped parsley
2 teaspoons chopped fennel or pinch dried fennel	2 teaspoons chopped fennel or pinch dried fennel
3 oz. soft breadcrumbs	75 g. soft breadcrumbs
seasoning	seasoning
2 tablespoons sherry or lemon juice	2 tablespoons sherry or lemon juice
Sauce:	*Sauce:*
$\frac{1}{2}$ pint thin cream	250 ml. thin cream
grated rind and juice of 1 lemon	grated rind and juice of 1 lemon
6–8 oz. small button mushrooms	150–200 g. small button mushrooms
2 tablespoons olive oil	2 tablespoons olive oil
Garnish:	*Garnish:*
parsley	parsley
few unshelled prawns	few unshelled prawns

1. Either mince the salmon, white fish and shelled prawns, or chop finely.
2. Make a thick sauce, heat the butter in a saucepan, add the flour, cook for several minutes, then add the milk, bring to the boil, cook until thickened.
3. Stir in the fish, eggs, herbs and crumbs, taste and season very well, add sherry or lemon juice.
4. Grease the tin, press in the mixture, bake until firm. For crisp sides as in the picture do not stand in a tin of water. Cover the fish mixture with greased foil or greaseproof paper.
5. Meanwhile blend the cream with the grated lemon rind and juice, season well.
6. Fry the mushrooms in oil, drain and add to the cream. Turn out the loaf, serve hot or cold with sauce, and garnish with parsley and prawns.

Crêpes d'épinards

Cooking time: 25 minutes
Preparation time: 20 minutes
Main cooking utensils: frying pan, 2 saucepans, flameproof dish,
   grill
Serves: 10–12

Imperial	Metric
Batter:	*Batter:*
6 oz. flour, preferably plain	150 g. flour, preferably plain
pinch salt	pinch salt
2 eggs	2 eggs
$\frac{1}{2}$ pint milk	250 ml. milk
6 tablespoons water	6 tablespoons water
1 tablespoon olive oil	1 tablespoon olive oil
oil or fat for frying	oil or fat for frying
Filling and topping:	*Filling and topping:*
2 12-oz. packets frozen	2 340-g. packets frozen
chopped spinach	chopped spinach
2 onions	2 onions
3 oz. butter or margarine	75 g. butter or margarine
3 oz. flour	75 g. flour
milk (see stage 8)	milk (see stage 8)
8 oz. cooked ham	200 g. cooked ham
2 oz. grated Cheddar or	50 g. grated Cheddar or
Gruyère cheese	Gruyère cheese

1. Sieve the flour and salt, beat in the eggs, milk and water until a smooth batter is formed.

2. Add the oil and beat again just before cooking.

3. Heat a little oil or fat in the pan and pour in sufficient batter to give a thin coating.

4. Cook on one side until golden brown, turn and cook on the second side.

5. Keep the pancakes hot on a dish over very hot water or in a slow oven.

6. Meanwhile cook the spinach in one pan, as shown on the packet, season well; strain, reserving liquid.

7. Chop the onions and fry in the hot butter or margarine until tender in the second pan, stir in the flour and cook for 2–3 minutes.

8. Measure the spinach liquid, add enough milk to give $1\frac{1}{4}$ pints (625 ml.), stir gradually into the flour, etc., and continue cooking until thick and smooth.

9. Add the cooked spinach and chopped ham.

10. Sandwich the pancakes with the spinach mixture, top with cheese and melt the cheese under a hot grill. Cut into wedges to serve.

Variation

Omit the ham and add grated cheese.

Mushroom pasties

Cooking time: 30 minutes
Preparation time: 45 minutes plus time for pastry to stand
   (10 minutes only if using frozen puff pastry)
Main cooking utensils: baking tray, saucepan
Oven temperature: very hot (475°F., 240°C., Gas Mark 9)
   then moderate (375°F., 190°C., Gas Mark 5)
Oven position: just above centre
Serves: 6–8

Imperial	Metric
Pastry:	*Pastry:*
8 oz. flour, preferably plain	200 g. flour, preferably plain
pinch salt	pinch salt
2 teaspoons lemon juice	2 teaspoons lemon juice
cold water	cold water
8 oz. butter	200 g. butter
Glaze:	*Glaze:*
beaten egg	beaten egg
Filling:	*Filling:*
8 oz. mushrooms	200 g. mushrooms
½ pint stock or milk	250 ml. stock or milk
seasoning	seasoning
1 oz. flour	25 g. flour
2 oz. butter	50 g. butter
grated rind of ½ lemon	grated rind of ½ lemon

1. Sieve the flour and salt, bind with the lemon juice and water, to form an elastic dough.

2. Roll out to a neat oblong, put the butter on the top, and fold pastry over the butter.

3. Turn, seal ends, 'rib' the pastry, roll out.

4. Fold in 3, turn, seal ends, 'rib' again and roll out.

5. Continue until the pastry has had 7 foldings and 7 rollings, put into a cool place between rollings.

6. When ready to make vol-au-vent cases, roll to $\frac{1}{3}$-inch ($\frac{1}{2}$-cm.) thickness, cut into 6—8 squares or oblongs, press a small cutter halfway through the pastry (leave a rim of $\frac{1}{3}$—$\frac{1}{2}$ inch ($\frac{1}{2}$ cm.) round this).

7. Glaze with beaten egg, bake until crisp and golden brown, about 15 minutes. Remove the lids and replace the pastry in a cooler oven to dry out.

8. Slice the mushrooms (unless very small), simmer in half the stock or milk until tender, season well.

9. Blend the flour with the remaining liquid, add to the pan with the butter and lemon rind and cook until thickened, stirring.

10. Put the filling in the pastry just before serving (use a little more flour if a thicker sauce is preferred).

Variation

Use frozen pastry — 1 lb. ($\frac{1}{2}$ kg.).

Skewered bacon in crumbs

Cooking time: 2 minutes
Preparation time: 10 minutes
Main cooking utensils: 4 skewers, pan for oil, absorbent paper
Serves: 4

Imperial	Metric
4 slices toast or plain rolls	4 slices toast or plain rolls
2 portions of mushroom-flavoured Camembert cheese or other cheese and about 8 tiny mushrooms (see variation)	2 portions of mushroom-flavoured Camembert cheese or other cheese and about 8 tiny mushrooms (see variation)
4 oz. boiled ham, cut in one piece	100 g. boiled ham, cut in one piece
paprika	paprika
little milk (about $\frac{1}{4}$ pint)	little milk (about 125 ml.)
Coating:	*Coating:*
2 eggs	2 eggs
1 oz. flour	25 g. flour
2 oz. fine breadcrumbs	50 g. fine breadcrumbs
To fry:	*To fry:*
oil	oil
To serve:	*To serve:*
tomato ketchup	tomato ketchup
salad	salad

1. Cut the toast or rolls into neat squares.
2. Divide the cheese into pieces, also the ham.
3. Put the toast or rolls, cheese and ham on to skewers, dusting the cheese with paprika.
4. Put a little milk in a shallow dish, lay the skewers on it and turn round in the milk for about 5 minutes.
5. Lift out, brush all the squares with beaten egg and coat well in flour then crumbs; this is particularly important for the cheese.
6. Fry in hot oil for 1–2 minutes only.
7. Lift out and drain. Serve on a dish with tomato ketchup as a dip, or as a light meal with the ketchup and salad.

Note: These may be served as a light meal, but if put on small skewers, so they can be eaten without difficulty, they are suitable for appetisers.

Variation

If mushroom-flavoured cheese is not available, put tiny mushrooms on skewers with plain cheese.

Cheese vols-au-vent

Cooking time: 15 minutes
Preparation time: 35 minutes plus time for pastry to stand
Main cooking utensils: flat baking tray, saucepan
Oven temperature: hot to very hot (450–475°F., 230–240°C.,
  Gas Mark 8–9)
Oven position: centre
Makes: 6 large or 12–18 small cases

Imperial	Metric
Puff pastry:	*Puff pastry:*
8 oz. plain flour	200 g. plain flour
pinch salt	pinch salt
water	water
little lemon juice	little lemon juice
8 oz. butter	200 g. butter
Cheese fondue:	*Cheese fondue:*
8 oz. grated cheese, two-thirds Gruyère and one-third Emmenthal	200 g. grated cheese, two-thirds Gruyère and one-third Emmenthal
shake pepper	shake pepper
paprika	paprika
grated nutmeg	grated nutmeg
1 teaspoon cornflour	1 teaspoon cornflour
$\frac{1}{2}$ clove garlic, crushed	$\frac{1}{2}$ clove garlic, crushed
1 teaspoon lemon juice	1 teaspoon lemon juice
just under $\frac{1}{4}$ pint dry white wine	just under 125 ml. dry white wine

1. To make puff pastry, sieve the flour and salt. Mix to a rolling consistency with water and lemon juice, roll out to an oblong shape; put 8 oz. (200 g.) butter on this. Fold in 3, turn, seal edges; 'rib' then roll out. Give total of 7 rollings and 7 foldings, putting away in a cool place between rollings.

2. To make vol-au-vent cases, roll out pastry to about $\frac{3}{4}$ inch. (1$\frac{1}{2}$ cm.) thick and cut into rounds.

3. Using a smaller cutter, mark out smaller rings in the centre of each round, cutting halfway through the pastry.

4. Bake until golden, lift out the centres, return to the oven for a few minutes, to dry out, if necessary.

5. To make the fondue, mix the dry ingredients together, add the lemon juice and wine.

6. Cook in a thick-bottomed pan over a low flame until the cheese is melted and it is a creamy liquid, or use a fondue set.

7. Pour mixture into vol-au-vent cases.

8. Serve hot, topped with pastry lids, or allow mixture to cool and fill the cold pastry cases, or top with a poached egg, see picture, and parsley.

Tomatoes with savoury egg filling

Cooking time: 15 minutes
Preparation time: 15 minutes
Main cooking utensils: ovenproof dish, 2 saucepans
Oven temperature: moderately hot (400°F., 200°C., Gas Mark 6)
Oven position: above centre
Serves: 4

Imperial	Metric
8 large firm tomatoes	8 large firm tomatoes
2–3 tablespoons finely chopped spring onions or grated onion	2–3 tablespoons finely chopped spring onions or grated onion
2 oz. butter	50 g. butter
seasoning	seasoning
2 oz. grated Dutch cheese	50 g. grated Dutch cheese
4 eggs	4 eggs
2 tablespoons thick cream	2 tablespoons thick cream
Garnish:	*Garnish:*
chopped parsley or chives	chopped parsley or chives
paprika pepper (optional)	paprika pepper (optional)

1. Cut the tops of the tomatoes, scoop out the centre pulp, dice the tomato 'lids'.
2. Blend the tomato pulp with the chopped onion and 1 oz. (25 g.) butter and heat for 4–5 minutes, season well, add the grated cheese.
3. Put back into the seasoned tomato cases and bake for 10 minutes.
4. Put the remaining butter into a saucepan and melt.
5. Beat the egg yolks and cream, season, fold in the stiffly beaten egg whites.
6. Cook in the hot butter until lightly set.
7. Pile on to the tomato cases and garnish. Serve as an hors d'oeuvre or light main dish.

Note: To save time, use 1 oz. (25 g.) ready grated Parmesan cheese and scramble the eggs in the usual way, do not separate.

Variation

Another simple way of combining eggs and tomatoes is to scoop out the tomato pulp, season well, mix with beaten egg and grated cheese and set in the oven.

Crab and cheese soufflé

Cooking time: 25–30 minutes
Preparation time: 20 minutes
Main cooking utensils: large pan, soufflé dish
Oven temperature: moderate (350–375°F., 180–190°C.,
  Gas Mark 4–5)
Oven position: centre
Serves: 4–5

Imperial	Metric
1 oz. butter	25 g. butter
½ oz. flour	15 g. flour
¼ pint milk	125 ml. milk
3 egg yolks	3 egg yolks
seasoning	seasoning
little cayenne pepper	little cayenne pepper
4 oz. crab meat	100 g. crab meat
2 oz. Parmesan cheese	50 g. Parmesan cheese
4 egg whites	4 egg whites

1. Make a sauce by melting the butter in a large pan, stirring in the flour and cooking slowly for a minute.
2. Gradually add the milk, return to the heat, stir vigorously over a moderate heat until the sauce thickens.
3. Cool a little, stir in the beaten egg yolks, seasoning and cayenne pepper. Add the flaked crab meat and finely grated cheese.
4. Whip the egg whites until stiff, fold carefully into the egg and crab mixture.
5. Turn into a buttered soufflé dish, bake for about 25–30 minutes, or until risen and brown. Serve at once either as an hors d'oeuvre or light main dish.

Variations
Use flaked smoked haddock in place of crab.
Cheese soufflé: Use 4 oz. (100 g.) cheese – all Parmesan or half Parmesan and half Gruyère.

Scallops in cheese sauce

Cooking time: 20 minutes
Preparation time: 15 minutes
Main cooking utensils: saucepan or saucepans, scallop shells
Serves: 4

Imperial	Metric
4 large or 8 small scallops	4 large or 8 small scallops
generous ½ pint milk	generous 250 ml. milk
seasoning	seasoning
1 oz. flour	25 g. flour
1 oz. butter	25 g. butter
little extra milk or cream (optional)	little extra milk or cream (optional)
3–4 oz. grated Gruyère or Cheddar cheese	75–100 g. grated Gruyère or Cheddar cheese
Garnish:	*Garnish:*
parsley	parsley
lemon	lemon

1. Remove the scallops from the shells; save any liquid that comes from beneath the fish and add this to the milk.
2. Either cook the orange roes with the white part of the fish or remove these and cook separately in a little salted water.
3. Put the scallops, whole or cut into fairly large pieces, into the milk, season lightly and simmer gently for 10 minutes. Test to see if they are tender.
4. Remove from the liquid and put on to the shells.
5. Blend the flour and butter together and add bit by bit to the milk, stirring well. Alternatively blend the flour with a little extra milk and add the milk together with the butter.
6. Bring to the boil and cook until the sauce is thick and smooth. Add the cheese and simmer gently for 1–2 minutes, taste and season.
7. Pour over the scallops, add the roes.
8. If necessary, heat for a few minutes under the grill. Serve with parsley and lemon.

Mussels in white wine

Cooking time: 25 minutes
Preparation time: 25 minutes
Main cooking utensils: 2 good-sized saucepans
Serves: 6 as an hors d'oeuvre or 4 as a main dish

Imperial	Metric
at least 4 pints mussels	at least 2¼ litres mussels
1 onion	1 onion
bouquet garni	bouquet garni
½ pint white wine	300 ml. white wine
seasoning	seasoning
Sauce:	*Sauce:*
1½ oz. butter or margarine	40 g. butter or margarine
1½ oz. flour	40 g. flour
1–2 teaspoons curry powder	1–2 teaspoons curry powder
¾ pint milk or half milk and half white wine	375 ml. milk or half milk and half white wine
2 tablespoons thick cream (optional)	2 tablespoons thick cream (optional)
seasoning	seasoning
Garnish:	*Garnish:*
parsley	parsley

1. Scrub the mussels well and wash in plenty of cold water, discard any whose shells are open and will not close when tapped sharply.
2. Put the mussels into the pan with the onion; leave this whole if not required in the sauce or chop finely if you wish to add it to the final dish.
3. Put in the bouquet garni, wine and seasoning and simmer steadily until the shells open.
4. Lift the fish out of the pan when cool enough to handle, pull off one shell, and cut away any weed-like growths.
5. Heat the butter or margarine, stir in the flour and curry powder, cook for several minutes, then blend in the milk and bring to the boil.
6. Add the strained liquid from the mussel pan and the cream and season well. Replace the mussels and heat. Serve on large plates, garnished with parsley.

Soufflé with poached eggs

Cooking time: 30 minutes
Preparation time: 20 minutes
Main cooking utensils: 2 saucepans, soufflé dishes
Oven temperature: moderate (375°F., 190°C., Gas Mark 5)
Serves: 4

Imperial	Metric
4 eggs	4 eggs
seasoning	seasoning
Soufflé mixture:	*Soufflé mixture:*
1 oz. butter	25 g. butter
1 oz. flour	25 g. flour
12 tablespoons milk	12 tablespoons milk
3 egg yolks	3 egg yolks
4 oz. finely grated	100 g. finely grated
Gruyère cheese	Gruyère cheese
5 egg whites	5 egg whites

1. Poach the eggs in boiling, salted water until set enough to handle; do not overcook.
2. Melt the butter in a pan, stir in the flour and cook for several minutes.
3. Gradually blend in the milk, bring to the boil and cook until thickened.
4. Season well, add the egg yolks and finely grated cheese.
5. Gradually fold in the stiffly beaten egg whites.
6. Put half the mixture into the greased soufflé dishes, top with the well-drained, poached eggs, then the rest of the soufflé mixture.
7. Bake for approximately 20 minutes until just set.

Note: This dish is equally suitable for an hors d'oeuvre or a savoury. Serve as soon as possible after cooking. This is eaten with a dessertspoon and fork.

Variation
Use a mixture of Parmesan and Cheddar cheese.

Mushrooms in cheese sauce

Cooking time: 15 minutes
Preparation time: 15 minutes
Main cooking utensils: frying pan, saucepan, grill pan
Serves: 6

Imperial	**Metric**
5 oz. mushrooms (button type)	150 g. mushrooms (button type)
4 oz. butter	100 g. butter
½ oz. flour	40 g. flour
½ pint milk	375 ml. milk
4 oz. lean, cooked ham	100 g. lean, cooked ham
seasoning	seasoning
5 oz. grated Gruyère,	125 g. grated Gruyère,
Emmenthal or Cheddar cheese	Emmenthal or Cheddar cheese
6 small slices bread	6 small slices bread
butter	butter
Garnish:	*Garnish:*
lettuce	lettuce
chopped parsley	chopped parsley

1. Slice mushrooms — do not peel if they are really good quality, for much of the flavour is in the skin. Wash and dry well.
2. Fry in half the hot butter, drain well when they are just tender.
3. Heat the rest of the butter in the saucepan, stir in the flour and cook for several minutes.
4. Gradually blend in the milk, bring to the boil, cook until thickened.
5. Add the diced ham, seasoning, the mushrooms and finally 4 oz. (100 g.) of the grated cheese. Do not stir too much as the mushroom juice spoils the colour of the sauce.
6. Do not over-cook once the cheese has been added.
7. Put the mixture on to slices of hot buttered toast, sprinkle with the remaining grated cheese and brown under the grill. Garnish and serve at once.

Leek savoury

Cooking time: 20 minutes
Preparation time: 15 minutes
Main cooking utensils: frying pan, grill pan, saucepan
Serves: 4

Imperial	Metric
4 large or 8 small leeks	4 large or 8 small leeks
2–3 oz. butter or margarine	50–75 g. butter or margarine
2–3 eggs	2–3 eggs
4 slices bread	4 slices bread
2 tomatoes	2 tomatoes
Garnish:	*Garnish:*
chopped parsley	chopped parsley
tomato ketchup	tomato ketchup

1. Wash leeks in cold water, particularly between leaves.
2. Discard the top of the leeks (use just the white part). The tender green parts could be used in soups or stews.
3. Cut the leeks into neat rings.
4. Heat the butter or margarine and toss the rings of leek in this, lower the heat and allow to cook gently and slowly.
5. Meanwhile hard-boil the eggs, crack the shells and put the eggs into cold water, this prevents a dark ring forming round the yolks.
6. When the leeks are nearly cooked, toast the bread and fry the sliced tomatoes slightly, or use raw tomatoes.
7. Pile the leeks on the hot toast, buttering it if wished.
8. Arrange sliced eggs and tomatoes on the dish.
9. Garnish with chopped parsley and a little ketchup. Serve as an hors d'oeuvre or savoury for an informal meal.

Cauliflower with cheese sauce

Cooking time: 25 minutes
Preparation time: 15 minutes
Main cooking utensils: 2 saucepans, serving dish or 4–6 scallop shells
Serves: 4–6

Imperial	Metric
½ pint milk	250 ml. milk
small pieces carrot	small pieces carrot
onion	onion
celery	celery
1 small cauliflower	1 small cauliflower
6–8 oz. young carrots	150–200 g. young carrots
seasoning	seasoning
Sauce:	*Sauce:*
1½ oz. butter	40 g. butter
1 oz. flour	25 g. flour
milk (see stage 1)	milk (see stage 1)
¼ pint vegetable stock	125 ml. vegetable stock
3 oz. grated Cheddar or	75 g. grated Cheddar or
Gruyère cheese	Gruyère cheese
Topping:	*Topping:*
2 oz. grated cheese	50 g. grated cheese
1 oz. soft breadcrumbs	25 g. soft breadcrumbs

1. Infuse the milk with the carrots, onion and celery by warming this, then letting it stand for about 30 minutes in a warm place; strain and use for the sauce.
2. Divide the cauliflower into neat sprigs and slice the carrots thinly.
3. Boil together in boiling, salted water until just tender.
4. Drain carefully and retain about $\frac{1}{4}$ pint (125 ml.) of the stock.
5. Heat the butter, stir in the flour and cook for several minutes.
6. Gradually blend in the milk and vegetable stock and bring to the boil, cook until thick and smooth.
7. Season well and add the cheese.
8. Put the hot vegetables into the dish or scallop shells.
9. Top with the sauce, sprinkle with cheese and crumbs and brown for a few minutes under a hot grill.

Note: It is a good idea to mix crumbs with cheese for topping as it prevents the cheese becoming 'stringy'.

Scrambled eggs and shrimps

Cooking time: few minutes
Preparation time: 10 minutes plus time for dried shrimps to stand
Main cooking utensil: saucepan
Serves: 6

Imperial	Metric
about 4 oz. dried shrimps (see note)	about 100 g. dried shrimps (see note)
6 eggs	6 eggs
seasoning	seasoning
pinch monosodium glutamate (see note)	pinch monosodium glutamate (see note)
pinch powdered ginger	pinch powdered ginger
2–3 spring onions	2–3 spring onions
2 tablespoons vegetable oil	2 tablespoons vegetable oil
Garnish:	Garnish:
chopped parsley or spring onion (green part)	chopped parsley or spring onion (green part)
few shrimps	few shrimps

1. If using the authentic Chinese dried shrimps, cover these with boiling water, leave for about 5–8 minutes and drain well. But if using fresh shrimps just shell them.
2. Beat the eggs with seasoning, add a pinch of monosodium glutamate, a pinch powdered ginger and the finely chopped white part of the spring onions.
3. Heat the oil in a pan, add the shrimps, heat thoroughly, then stir in the egg mixture and continue cooking until the eggs are lightly set. Garnish with chopped parsley or the chopped green part of spring onion and shrimps.

Note: Normally this mixture would be served as part of a Chinese meal, but it makes an excellent hors d'oeuvre put on to toast and served separately. Tiny fingers of toast could be topped with the mixture to serve with drinks. Dried shrimps and monosodium glutamate are available from Chinese food stores.

Stuffed tomatoes and peppers

Cooking time: see methods
Preparation time: 30 minutes
Main cooking utensils: frying pan, ovenproof dish
Oven temperature: moderate to moderately hot (375–400°F., 190–200°C., Gas Mark 5–6)
Oven position: just above centre
Serves: 4

Stuffed tomatoes

Imperial	Metric
4 very large tomatoes or 8 smaller tomatoes	4 very large tomatoes or 8 smaller tomatoes
5 oz. mushrooms	150 g. mushrooms
1 clove garlic	1 clove garlic
4 tablespoons oil	4 tablespoons oil
½ tablespoon chopped parsley	½ tablespoon chopped parsley
4 oz. grated cheese	100 g. grated cheese
seasoning	seasoning

1. Remove the tops from the tomatoes (the ones in the picture are very large Italian tomatoes) and scoop out the pulp.
2. Mix with the chopped mushrooms, crushed garlic fried in oil, chopped parsley, cheese and seasoning.
3. Bake for 15 minutes.

Stuffed peppers

Imperial	Metric
4 red peppers	4 red peppers
2 onions	2 onions
2 cloves garlic	2 cloves garlic
3 tomatoes	3 tomatoes
3–4 tablespoons oil	3–4 tablespoons oil
¼ pint water	150 ml. water
2–3 oz. bread (crustless)	50–75 g. bread (crustless)
seasoning	seasoning
4 small mackerel	4 small mackerel
2 oz. grated cheese	50 g. grated cheese

1. Cut a slice from the top of each pepper, scoop out the centre core and seeds, chop the top slices finely.
2. Fry the chopped onions, crushed garlic, tomatoes and chopped peppers in hot oil.
3. Pour water over the bread, leave for 10 minutes, beat until smooth, add to the onions and tomatoes, season.
4. Turn the pepper cases in oil in the pan for several minutes until slightly softened on the outside.
5. Put the onion mixture at the bottom of the cases, top with the diced raw mackerel (or other fish), cover with cheese.
6. Bake in an oiled dish for 25 minutes until fish and peppers are tender. Garnish with parsley or celery leaves if liked.

Mixed hors d'oeuvre

These five recipes may be served individually but together they make a splendid hors d'oeuvre for 8–12 people. Arrange them on an hors d'oeuvre tray or on five individual serving dishes.

Spanish salad
Boil 4 oz. (100 g.) long-grain rice in well-seasoned water until just soft, drain, mix with 4–5 tablespoons mayonnaise while still hot; add 8 oz. (200 g.) cooked peas, 1 diced red and 1 diced green pepper (discard cores and seeds). Add several diced stuffed olives, 2–3 neatly diced tomatoes and 6–8 chopped spring onions.

Curried eggs
Hard-boil, shell and halve 4–6 eggs. Blend together 1 teaspoon curry powder, 4 tablespoons mayonnaise, and 1–2 teaspoons horseradish cream. Arrange the halved eggs on a bed of lettuce, coat with the above dressing, garnish with finely chopped parsley, twists of cucumber and tomato.

Seafood
Blend the meat flaked from 1 small cooked crab or a can of crab meat with 4–6 oz. (100–150 g.) cooked or canned salmon, 4 oz. (100 g.) shelled prawns, a little diced celery and diced cucumber and 4 tablespoons mayonnaise. Add lemon juice to moisten. Garnish with lemon slices.

Chef's salad
Cut 4–6 oz. (100–150 g.) cooked ham, 4–6 oz. (100–150 g.) cooked tongue, 4–6 oz. (100–150 g.) Gruyère cheese into fine matchstick shreds. Blend with 2–3 tablespoons mayonnaise and 3 oz. (75 g.) chopped shelled fresh or dried walnuts and the segments from 2 oranges. Serve on lettuce, top with slices from 1 orange and 1 oz. (25 g.) chopped walnuts.

Beetroot and apple
Cut 1 large cooked peeled beetroot and 2–3 peeled dessert apples into neat pieces, blend with a few finely chopped spring onions, 1 tablespoon olive oil, 1 tablespoon vinegar and seasoning.

Mixed salad

Preparation time: 10 minutes
Main cooking utensils: bowls, saucepan (see stage 6)
Serves: 4–6

Imperial	Metric
1 pickled herring (rollmop or Bismarck)	1 pickled herring (rollmop or Bismarck)
1 apple	1 apple
2 oz. raisins	50 g. raisins
little made mustard	little made mustard
1 tablespoon oil	1 tablespoon oil
½ tablespoon vinegar	½ tablespoon vinegar
small piece German garlic sausage or cooked sausage	small piece German garlic sausage or cooked sausage
2–3 tomatoes	2–3 tomatoes
4 oz. cooked peas	100 g. cooked peas
small can asparagus	small can asparagus
mayonnaise	mayonnaise
small cauliflower	small cauliflower
2 oz. mushrooms	50 g. mushrooms
2 oz. cooked ham or bacon	50 g. cooked ham or bacon
2–3 sticks celery	2–3 sticks celery
little soured cream or mayonnaise	little soured cream or mayonnaise
seasoning	seasoning
Garnish:	*Garnish:*
cheese or chicken	cheese or chicken
peas	peas
apple	apple
celery leaves	celery leaves

1. Drain the herring, use the vinegar for the sauce if wished.

2. Chop the fish into very small pieces, mix with the diced but not peeled apple and raisins.

3. Blend the mustard with the oil and vinegar, mix with the ingredients above and put into the dish.

4. Dice the sausage, cut the tomatoes into neat pieces.

5. Blend with the peas, asparagus and mayonnaise, put into a dish.

6. Either use the cauliflower raw, or cook lightly for a few minutes only.

7. Blend with sliced, well washed, raw mushrooms, chopped ham and celery, and bind with soured cream or mayonnaise. Season very well, put into dish. Top with garnishes and serve at once.

Note: Also in this picture is an easy savoury, hot buttered toast topped with tuna fish, egg and olives.

Vitamin hors d'oeuvre

Preparation time: 20 minutes
Main utensil: bowl
Serves: 4–6

Imperial	Metric
about 12 oz. sauerkraut	about 300 g. sauerkraut
1 small onion	1 small onion
4–5 bananas	4–5 bananas
juice of 2 lemons	juice of 2 lemons
1–2 cans mandarin oranges	1–2 cans mandarin oranges
or about 6 fresh mandarins	or about 6 fresh mandarins
2–3 heads chicory	2–3 heads chicory
seasoning	seasoning
2 young leeks	2 young leeks
1–2 tablespoons vegetable oil	1–2 tablespoons vegetable oil
1 large or 2 small heads fennel	1 large or 2 small heads fennel
3 oz. raisins	75 g. raisins
1 oz. desiccated coconut	25 g. desiccated coconut

1. Drain and wash the sauerkraut well, allow to dry on a clean cloth, then flavour with finely chopped onion. If preferred, cook the sauerkraut then flavour with onion, blend with sliced bananas, lemon juice and mandarin oranges.

2. Shred well-washed and dried chicory, blend with bananas, lemon juice, seasoning and mandarin oranges.

3. Shred raw leeks very finely, using all the white part and some of the most tender green, blend with oil, lemon juice, seasoning and mandarin oranges.

4. Chop fennel well (soak in cold water for a while to make crisp), blend with raisins, mandarin oranges and coconut.

Note: Serve any or all of these salads with crispbread and butter or as a main dish with cheese or eggs.

Goblet salads

Preparation time: 20 minutes
Serves: 4

This way of serving a salad is particularly suitable for a buffet, as it can be eaten with a spoon or small fork. It can either form an hors d'oeuvre or part of a main course.

Salade de fromage et salami

Pull the leaves of a small lettuce heart apart, wash and dry, then shred coarsely and put into the bottom of the serving glasses or dishes. Drain a small can of asparagus tips and chop if wished, slice 2–3 small, raw button mushrooms neatly and cut 8 oz. (200 g.) Gruyère cheese into thick matchsticks. Mix together with 1–2 teaspoons capers and 1 oz. (25 g.) grated Parmesan cheese and put into the dishes. Moisten with dressing made by blending 3 tablespoons olive oil, salt, pepper, dry mustard and 1½ tablespoons lemon juice or vinegar together. Top with cones of salami, black olives and sprigs of parsley.

Salade parisienne

This French salad is another mixture of ingredients that could be served in a similar way to the cheese and salami salad. Cut 12 oz. (300 g.) mixed cooked meat (veal, tongue, ham or beef) into matchstick pieces, chop 2 hard-boiled eggs and dice 8 oz. (200 g.) potatoes. Mix together with a finely chopped or grated onion and put on a bed of shredded lettuce. Top with dressing, as above, and garnish with chopped chervil or parsley.

Acknowledgements

The following photographs are by courtesy of:

Birds Eye Frozen Foods Limited: page 92
British Egg Information Service: pages 88, 102
California Prune Advisory Bureau: page 86
Champignon Käsewerk, Limited (Germany): page 96
Dutch Fruit and Vegetable Producers' Association: pages 14, 18, 20, 58, 94, 100, 112
Electricity Council: page 66
Fruit Producers' Council: pages 38, 50, 82
Gales Honey: page 68
Isleworth Polytechnic: page 40
Italian Lemons: page 76
Karl Ostmann, Limited (Germany): pages 16, 28, 32, 34, 42, 46, 52, 62
Lawry's Foods International Inc.: page 54
Plumrose Limited: page 80
Potato Marketing Board: page 30
'Pyrosil' – Jobling Housecraft Service: page 10
Spanish Melons: page 70
Stork Cookery Service: page 56
Swiss Cheese Union: pages 64, 98, 126